RE

DISCIPLESHIP

THE QUEST
31 REFLECTIONS ON AUTHENTIC DISCIPLESHIP

RON BENNETT

ACKNOWLEDGEMENTS

Unless otherwise noted all Scripture taken from the New American Standard Bible©, copyright ©1960, 1962, 1963, 1968, 1971, 1972, 1973, 19775, 1977, 1995 by the Lockman Foundation. Used by permission.

Scripture quotations marked MSG are taken from THE MES-SAGE, copyright© 1993, 1994, 1995, 1996, 2000, 2001, 2002 by Eugene Peterson. Used by permission of NavPress. All rights reserved. Represented by Tyndale house publishers, Inc.

Scripture quotations marked NLT are taken from the New Living Translation, copyright ©1996, 2004, 2007, 20013, 2015 by Tyndale Charitable Trust. All rights reserved, Used by permission.

Cover design by Matt Heflin

Special thanks to my wife, Mary, for her support, encouragement, and editing.

REVIEWS

Ron's "Reflections" have helped clarified my understanding of discipleship in a way that both encourages and motivates me. His use of metaphors makes truth relevant and practical.

Becky Sorensen
Elementary Teacher

No one lives, breathes, and dissects biblical discipleship more than Ron Bennett. Combined with his fascinating use of creative illustrations, every word you read will take you on an adventure in discipleship. Get ready to be challenged and blessed!

Don Miller
Lead Pastor, Westover Church

Ron's powerful, biblically-based and real-life insights provide invaluable perspective and encouragement to Christ-followers who share Ron's desire to grow in the capacity to fully live the lives to which Jesus has invited us.

Crag Chval
Corporate Lawyer

Ron's Spirit-filled insights from Scripture have been a tremendous source of growth for me in my walk with Christ. His wisdom and gift of expression are a blessing to many.

Nick Wages
Senior Loan Consultant

I respond to the use of pictures that Ron uses to illustrate the teaching being presented. They open up the message and keep it fresh in my thoughts as I continue to read and learn.

Sharon Geiger
High School Nurse

Ron is not just a thought-leader in disciplemaking. He is an everyday practitioner whose life and work is shaped by his faith. Ron takes this "adventure of discipleship" to us every day, ordinary people in practical and easy ways, making it a "do-able adventure" with his ongoing help and wisdom.

Jack McQueeney,
The Navigators, The Apprentice Approach

As a non-biblical scholar, I find Ron's writings extremely impactful in my growth as a disciple and a disciple-maker. This collection of reflections will be a reference treasure for me.

Bill Penkethman
Owner, Custom Suit Yourself

Ron's writings have given me clarity and perspective on what Jesus meant when he said, "Follow me." It has been a beautiful thing that has assisted me and those I am discipling.

Trevis Wadlow
Owner, Wadlow Drywall Inc.

TABLE OF CONTENTS

Preface   3

Introduction   7

1. The Picture in Our Mind   11

2. Discipleship on the Resurrection Side of the Cross   15

3. Portrait of Discipleship   19

4. An Audience of One   23

5. The Fear Factor   27

6. Living the Wow   31

7. Highway Hazards   35

8. Real Life Monopoly   39

9. Flatland to Spaceland   43

10. Reducing Tension in Discipleship   47

11. The Day the Music Died   51

12. Gospel of the Gaps   55

13. Unintended Consequences   59

14.   Now Playing: His Story   63

15. The Incarnation   67

16. The Demonstration   71

17. The Crucifixion   75

18. The Resurrection   79

19. The Ascension   83

20. The Coronation   87

21. The Examination   91

22. Kingdoms in Conflict   95

23. The Cross and the Crown   99

24. Grace and Conditions   103

25. God's Iridescent Love   107

26. God's Refracted Love   113

27. God's Love Language   117

28. God's Reflected Love   121

29. Knowing is more than Knowledge   125

30. Free but not Automatic   129

31. What's on the Whiteboard?   133

PREFACE

The word "disciple" or "discipleship" is an archaic word mostly used today in religious circles. It is, however, a term used frequently in the Bible to identify those who were connected to the rabbi Jesus. You may have even heard it used to describe the mission Christ gave the eleven apostles just before his ascension: to go and make disciples, commonly referred to as the Great Commission.

It is a word used primarily in the four Gospels and the book of Acts. The early church community saw it as their mandate to make disciples throughout the Roman Empire (Acts1:8). The word described not only converts to Christianity but also the life change that identified these believers as belonging to The Way. They reflected the values, character, mission, attitudes, and behavior of the Rabbi Jesus; they lived the way he did. The result was a community of people who distinctively imitated Christ.

Today, separated by 2000 years of history from the initial mission, we need to rethink our understanding of discipleship. Two observations will help make this point.

1. The general spiritual maturity of current believers is embarrassingly shallow. John Stott, worldwide preacher, evangelist, author, and Bible teacher, considered by Time magazine in 2005 to be among the "100 Most Influential People in the world, wrote his final book in 2010." The book, "The Radical Disciple" [1], was his farewell address to the church. In it he summarizes the condition of the worldwide Christian community as having "growth without depth," in other words, broad but shallow.

Willow Creek Church in Chicago provides a contemporary illustration. Around 2003, after having grown into a congregation of thousands, the church decided to assess their ministry regarding the fulfillment of their mission statement "to develop fully devoted followers of Christ." Their work turned into a national assessment tool called "Reveal." What they found about their ministry was common to the thousands of churches that courageously used this assessment tool.

One of their surpising discoveries was that higher levels of church activity did not predict long-term spiritual growth as measured by increasing love for God or increasing love for people. [2]

2. The second observation is that the word disciple or discipleship, when used in church cultures, is frequently ambiguous. Since "We cannot produce what we cannot describe"[3], perhaps this uncertainty has contributed to the shallow condition of present-day Christianity.

Over my 50 years of ministry, I have found that believers view a disciple with several mental pictures:

1. A Special Forces, Seal Team 6, kind of person who is highly dedicated - kind of a super Christian.

2. A Bible student/scholar who knows a lot about the Bible, frequently attending Bible studies and classes.

3. A "whatever" image in which anything a Christian is doing in the church qualifies him/her as a disciple.

On a personal level, what is your picture of discipleship? How would you finish the statement: A disciple is_____? More importantly, is your picture of discipleship anywhere close to the image Jesus had in mind when he called people to be his disciples?

The purpose of this book is to challenge our current under-

4

standing of discipleship, appealing to Scripture for clarity. Otherwise our culture (Christian or secular) will distort and redefine what the original Author had in mind. This rethinking and reexamining our current picture of discipleship, however, is not as easy as it may sound.

Recent studies of the brain and our cognitive functions have identified that cognition takes place in two separate areas of the brain: the conscious mind located in the front of our brain and the "cognitive unconscious" (CU) mind located near our brain stem. The CU is an automated storage facility, much like an art museum where we store pictures of concepts like father, mother, love, peace, God, Jesus, and discipleship. These pictures, developed over time, act as a filter for understanding and interpreting new information, especially information that does not fit our current image (schema).

Unlike the conscious mind, the CU mind is automated and fast. When information is received that causes cognitive dissonance because it does not fit our stored picture, we can do one of three things. We either automatically reject the new information as inaccurate and not worthy of consideration, or we try to modify the incoming data to fit our current picture. For example, a husband thinks, "When she said I was insensitive, she must just be having a bad day."

The third option is the most challenging but also essential if we are to make any progress in modifying our understanding. It requires taking the current picture out of the gallery of our CU and bringing it into the workroom of our conscious mind, where we wrestle with the cognitive dissonance and adjust our understanding before putting it back into our automated museum.

My invitation, as you read the following chapters, is to rethink/ reevaluate the current picture you have of discipleship. Bring this picture into the workroom of your conscious mind and reexamine it. As you wrestle, reflect, and meditate on what you read, see if it will not help bring clarity to this most crucial concept. Then, when you put your picture back into your mental museum, it may look more like the picture of discipleship that hangs in the gallery of Jesus's mind.

[1] *The Radical Disciple,* John Stott, IVP, p 38
[2] *Move,* Willow Creek Association, Zondervan p.18
[3] Dr. Robert Lewis

Introduction
The Quest

In 1804 Lewis and Clark, with about four dozen men, set out from St. Louis to find a waterway to America's west coast. Commissioned by President Jefferson, they were tasked with the mission to explore and discover an economical means of travel through the recently acquired Louisiana Purchase. Secondary purposes included mapping the territory, extending American influence, and making scientific discoveries.

Accomplishing their mission, the party returned to St Louis in 1806. Along the way, they made friends (and enemies), "took pictures," collected samples, and explored the breathtaking beauty of deserts, mountains, and rivers. But upon returning, the men took up life basically where they had left off, other than having some great memories and a more extensive scrapbook; life was the same. It was a trip…with adventure.

Several decades later, another group of men and women also left St. Louis for the west coast. Commonly called pioneers, these people had a different mission. They sold all they had, left the modern comforts of the 1840s, and headed west for a new life. With the transcontinental railroad still a couple of decades away, they had no plans for returning to their old life. It was a one-way ticket through the unknown to realize a dream. They had a dream that motivated them to risk all they had and invest in this epic adventure supported by both fact and fiction. Those that made the arduous journey were never the same.

The Lewis party made a trip, but it was more than a trip for the pioneers; it was a quest. The 1678 classic Christian allegory, "Pilgrim's Progress," written by John Bunyan (not related to Paul!), tells of another adventure that was a quest rather than a trip. The story follows Christian, the main character, along his journey to the Celestial City. Along the way he encountered various adventures that changed him forever and prepared him for his final destination.

Discipleship is a quest: a journey of no return. Along the way, we face multiple challenges, gaze at incredible vistas, and encounter unexpected opportunities, and we'll never be the same. We are not coming back to where we started. It is an adventure of surprising discovery, primarily of the One who placed the vertical heavenly tug on our hearts (Eccl. 3:11).

Authentic discipleship is not a course we take or a scrapbook we make. It is not something we complete and move on to the next challenge. The great Rabbi Yahshua has invited us to leave the familiar comforts, sell all we have, buy a Conestoga wagon, band together with fellow pioneers, and head west. With our confidence in Christ as our guide, we need never look back. Along the way, we will likely realize that we have taken too much luggage. Much that we initially thought essential, we will abandon. It's the stuff that no longer fits who we are or where we are going. And we won't miss it.

To those initial fishermen along the Sea of Galilee, Jesus gave an invitation to follow Him. That invitation still stands. It is an ongoing invitation to every generation to join His quest (Matt. 4:19). Paul expressed his journey as a quest in Phil 3:12-14.

I don't mean that I have already achieved these things or that I have already reached perfection. But I press on to possess that perfection for which Christ Jesus first possessed me. No, dear brothers and sisters, I have not achieved it, but I focus on this one thing: Forgetting the past and looking forward to what lies ahead, I press on to reach the end of the race and receive the heavenly prize for which God, through Christ Jesus, is calling us.

My purpose in the following material is not to be comprehensive but catalytic to your journey of discipleship. You can read one each day for a month requiring less than ten minutes per day. Better yet, read one and reflect on it, adding your observations before you move on to the next one. Even better, I would encourage you to read them with a partner and discuss your insights.

From the very first day, we were there, taking it all in—
we heard it with our own ears, saw it with our own eyes,
verified it with our own hands.
The Word of Life appeared right before our eyes;
we saw it happen!
And now we're telling you in most sober prose
that what we witnessed was, incredibly, this:
The infinite Life of God himself took shape before us.
We saw it, we heard it, and now we're telling you
so you can experience it along with us,
this experience of communion with the Father and his Son,
Jesus Christ.
Our motive for writing is simply this:
We want you to enjoy this, too.
Your joy will double our joy (1John 1:1-4 MSG)!

Welcome to the Quest!

1

The Picture in our Mind

Jesus called out to them, "Come, follow Me,
and I will show you how to fish for people! (Mat 4:19 NLT)

Words are stupid things, it's meaning that counts. Words are simply containers into which each of us packs meaning and mental pictures. Conversation uses shared words, but communication involves shared meanings.

We have all had the experience of using words to explain our idea to another person only to find out later that what we thought we said was not what the other person heard or understood. The key to communication is shared meaning, not words. For example, I may say wasser, and you may say aqua, but we communicate only if we both are thinking of H2O (water!).

This challenge in communication exists even when we speak the same language, live in the same culture, and inhabit the same historical period. In 2016 the Navigators asked the Barna organization to study the state of discipleship in America. In the published results, the opening statement succinctly states the problem.

"A critical component of this study is to define "discipleship." The concept is familiar to many, but a widely accepted definition remains elusive."

A more recent study came to the same conclusion:

Lack of commonly understood definitions – there is not a clear, compelling, and commonly understood set of basic definitions for terms such as discipleship, disciple, and disciple-making. This makes it very difficult to assess effectiveness within local churches and within the broader church community (consistent definitions do not prevail in Protestant churches in the USA). [1]

A few years ago, a friend of mine told me about a conversation he had with his five-year-old son. The dad told his son about an upcoming vacation in which they would travel to California. Along the way, they were going to stop and see the Grand Canyon and Hoover Dam. He then said to his son, "Do you know what a dam does?"

"Sure," his son replied, "A dam holds back water!"

"That's right," the dad proudly said, "But do you know that a dam also makes electricity?"

Without hesitation, the son replied, "Well, praise God for beavers!"

I would suggest that our cultural picture of discipleship is more like a beaver dam, but when Jesus used the term, he was thinking Hoover Dam.

The conclusion: communication is often difficult even with a common language. However, communication complexity increases exponentially when translating from a different language, foreign culture, and historical setting 2,000 years prior. Therefore, we must draw from the biblical context to understand what Jesus had in mind when he used the term "disciple."

A significant contributor to the confusion is that we translate our meaning of disciple from the Greek language used to write the New Testament manuscripts.

The Greek term for disciple is *mathetes*, which means student or pupil. According to this understanding, Jesus is a teacher, and we, his disciples, are simply learners. But Jesus was not a Greek; he was a Hebrew rabbi. The Greek meaning is not inaccurate, just incomplete. The Webster Online Dictionary captures the issue with their definition of a disciple:

A true disciple is not just a student or a learner, but a follower, one who applies what he has learned. Thus a true disciple will ask, 'What would Jesus do?

The Hebrew word for disciple is *talmidim*. In the first century Hebrew culture of Jesus' day, a disciple was a *talmidim* of a particular rabbi. A rabbi's *talmidim* not only sought to know what the rabbi knew but to replicate how the rabbi lived in every way possible. In other words, a Hebrew disciple is more like an apprentice who lives close to his mentor 24/7. Ray VanderLaan illustrates this by saying a disciple would walk so close to his rabbi that he would be "covered with the dust of his sandals" [2]

Since the Greek model of education has dramatically influenced our educational system today, our picture of a student/teacher relationship is a classroom with students taking notes. And that is the primary paradigm for our churches as well. Jesus, as a rabbi, certainly taught the crowds. However, the discipleship took place in the interpersonal intimacy of a small group of followers who wanted to know not only what the teacher knew but how to live their lives to be like their teacher in every way possible. A Hebrew disciple didn't attend lectures; he/she imitated the life of the rabbi.

Jesus gives us his picture of discipleship when he said, "A pupil (disciple) is not above his teacher; but everyone, after he has been fully trained, will be like his teacher" (Luke 6:40). The focus of discipleship with Jesus was his person: "follow me" (Matt. 4:19). When we reduce discipleship to information download, we distort the original picture, marginalizing transformation and robbing discipleship of its intended focus.

So I invite you to take down the picture of discipleship hanging in the gallery of your unconscious cognitive mind, bring it into the workroom of your conscious mind, and reexamine it. The purpose of the following chapters is to give you a fresh perspective to repaint your picture of discipleship.

[1] Discipleship.org/Grey Matter Research and Consulting, 2020 ("A National Study of Disciple Making in USA Churches: High Aspirations, Disappointing Results")

[2] "That the World May Know series", Focus on the Family

For Reflection

1. What is the current picture of discipleship that hangs in the gallery of your mind? How would you finish this statement: A disciple is……..?

2. Where did you get your current picture? How much of your image comes from cultural Christianity, and how much from Scripture?

2

Discipleship
on the Resurrection Side of the Cross

Yes, I am the vine; you are the branches.
Those who remain in Me, and I in them, will produce much fruit.
For apart from Me you can do nothing (John 15:5 NLT).

The biblical term "disciple" primarily comes from the New Testament Gospels; it has limited use in the book of Acts and is absent in the Epistles. However, I would suggest that the concept of discipleship permeates all of Scripture. Jesus built on the rich Hebrew heritage, and the apostles built on Jesus's example and teaching.

Old Testament

The term disciple is not an Old Testament word, but the concept is still there. Discipleship took place primarily in the context of the family (Deut. 6:6-9). Moses/Joshua and Elijah/Elisha are two of the few examples of one adult mentoring another.

However, the primary way discipleship occurs in the Old Testament is found in the history of God discipling his covenant family, the nation of Israel. They were his chosen people, and He was to be their God. What made their relationship unique was God's promise to be near them, illustrated by the Exodus, the wilderness journey, the tabernacle, and the establishment of a nation. The expected response was for God's people to seek him. Isaiah states this response succinctly, "Seek the LORD while He may be found; Call upon Him while He is near" (Isa. 55:6).

King David is a superlative example of Old Testament discipleship. God called David a man after the heart of God. "He raised up David to be their king, concerning whom He also testified and said, 'I HAVE FOUND DAVID the son of Jesse, A MAN AFTER MY HEART, who will do all My will'" (Acts 13:22 NASB). David's discipleship response was, "When You said, 'Seek My face' my heart said to You, 'Your face, O LORD, I shall seek'" (Psalm 27:8).

Gospels

As we begin the New Testament phase of the storyline, the paradigm of discipleship changes dramatically. God is no longer just near us; he is now physically with us. "It was prophesied that a virgin would give birth and he would be called "Immanuel" which means God is with us" (Matt. 1:23). Or, as John writes, "And the Word became flesh, and dwelt among us, and we saw His glory, glory as of the only begotten from the Father, full of grace and truth" (John 1:14).

The eternal God of the Old Testament entered our world in the form of a person, the Son of God/Son of Man, and walked among us. In the gospel period, discipleship was modeled by those physically with him, those who could hear, see, and touch him.

The closest to him were the 12 disciples chosen to be with him. "And He appointed twelve, so that they would be with Him and that He could send them out to preach" (Mark 3:14).

The responsive word for discipleship at this time in history was to follow him. The following was literal as well as figurative. There were concentric circles of disciples with increasing closeness to him: 70 who followed Jesus consistently, the 12 apostles who followed him closely and continuously, and three who were even closer to him. Only a few people had the opportunity to be in the Creator's presence to hear, walk, eat, and touch him.

Ascension

After the resurrection and ascension, discipleship enters a new phase. Jesus would no longer be physically present with his disciples. Instead, with the gift of the indwelling Holy Spirit, discipleship is now based on us being in him and he in us. The progression is an unbelievable intimacy proceeding from God being near, with, and now in-dwelling his people.

This new paradigm has enormous implications, including a relationship with Jesus, which he described as being like the connection between a vine and its branches. The responsive word to this "in him" discipleship is to abide. Just as the branch must remain intimately connected to the vine to bear fruit, so also we are to abide (intimately connected) in Christ to bear spiritual fruit (John 15). Paul describes this new relational dynamic as learning to walk in him (Col. 2:6). Both abiding and walking in Christ define discipleship on the resurrection side of the cross.

Another implication of discipleship after the ascension is our new identity in Christ. Faith in Christ transfers us not only from the kingdom of darkness to the kingdom of light but gives us a new distinctiveness – in Christ. "Therefore if anyone is in Christ, he is a new creature; the old things passed away; behold, new things have come" (2 Cor. 5:17).

Consider a few of the "new" things we now have because Christ is in us. Our identity in Christ includes a new:

- Spirit living within
- Covenant relationship with God
- Identity as a child of God
- Access to the Father
- Freedom to live for God
- Hope for eternal life
- Lord and loving master
- Destiny and purpose

- Spiritual family
- Home waiting in heaven

Discipleship today must consider all our resources in Christ, resources the initial disciples did not have nor could have imagined. Now discipleship is a relationship in which he is not just near or with us but actually in us. Discovering what that means and how to live it out in our daily lives is the great adventure of discipleship on the cross's resurrection side.

For Reflection

1. What other changes can you think of that affect discipleship on this side of the resurrection?

2. What are some implications of discipleship that come from the concept "seek my face" or "he set his face to seek the Lord"?

3

A Portrait of Discipleship

A pupil is not above his teacher;
but everyone, after he has been fully trained,
will be like his teacher (Luke 6:40).

The "Follow me" Jesus gave to the original disciples was more than a suggestion; it was a call to discipleship. This call echoes down through history. Men and women in every generation have heard it and followed. This same call remains in effect in our present-day and can serve as a succinct definition of a disciple: a follower of Christ.

After Christ's ascension the early disciples were recognized by their conduct as followers of Jesus. Luke tells us that even those opposed to Jesus identified these men as his imitators. "Now as [the religious leaders] observed the confidence of Peter and John and understood that they were uneducated and untrained men, they were amazed, and began to recognize them as having been with Jesus" (Acts 4:13, ESV). There was an undeniable imitation that was recognizable.

Are Christ's disciples recognizable today? Would those who observe our lives come to the same conclusion: he/she has been with Jesus?

Since we are on a journey to rethink the mental picture of discipleship that hangs in our mental museum, let me share the working description that currently reflects my mental image. This picture has been periodically assessed and repainted over the years. It is a work in progress; I continue to ask the question, "What was the picture of discipleship that Jesus had in his mind when he gave us the Great Commission?" If you don't have a current discipleship description, I offer mine as a starting point. Then as you study and reflect, see how well it holds up. Use it, modify it, or develop your own as you read through the reflections on discipleship in this book.

In Darwin's *Black Box,* Michael Behe uses the term "irreducible complexity." The concept describes the phenomenon in nature by which even a simple organism cannot function without all of its essential parts. If even one is missing, the organism is not viable. Here is my most recent, best shot at describing the irreducible complexity of discipleship:

Discipleship is the personal, persistent pursuit of knowing, reflecting, and sharing Christ utilizing critical spiritual disciplines in the context of supporting relationships in order to beomce his image bearer.

The following is a quick flyover of the description:

Discipleship is the personal, persistent pursuit...

Discipleship is an individual concept. There are no group disciples. Although done in a community, it is essentially an individual active pursuit that involves intentionality and effort. It will not happen without our cooperation and involvement. Jesus used the term "abide" in John 15 to express this critical relationship in which both his grace and our effort are connected (see Philippians 2:12-13).

It is a continual pursuit that requires choices every day. The command to abide is not an event or a program but rather a direction we travel.

It is not a place we attain and then quit. The Apostle Paul shares his journey of discipleship with the statement, "Not that I have already obtained it or have already become perfect, but I press on so that I may lay hold of that for which also I was laid hold of by Christ Jesus" (Phil. 3:12).

...of knowing, reflecting, and sharing Christ...

Knowing, reflecting, and sharing Christ are like the coordinates of our quest. It is our GPS setting. These three pursuits form a critical triad in which each contributes to and enhances the others. As we gain experiential knowledge of who Jesus is, we align ourselves to reflect that reality. As we model a clearer picture of who Jesus is, we represent him more accurately to the world around us.

...utilizing critical spiritual disciplines ...

Discipleship on the resurrection side of the cross must also consider its method of achievement. These means of grace are commonly called spiritual disciplines, habits, or practices. They are the God-ordained way by which we experience his grace. They are the way we "abide" in Christ so that we bear fruit by his power. They are, in the words of Dallas Willard, "what we do so God can do what we cannot do."

There is no comprehensive list of the spiritual disciplines, but certain ones have been practiced and promoted throughout Christian history. The most common spiritual habits in our church culture today are worship, connecting, and serving - all of which are outer disciplines. Although essential, by themselves, they are inadequate to produce authentic life transformation. There is, however, a set of inner disciplines that are historically proven effective for life transformation. These internal disciplines involve habits that connect us with Christ (prayer, Bible study) and those that disconnect us from the world around us (fasting, solitude).

...in the context of supporting relationships ...

Discipleship does not happen in isolation. In the New Testament, discipleship is modeled and taught as a pursuit of Christ in relationship with others on the same journey. Jesus had his small band of disciples; Paul had his. Paul gives us the most succinct description of these crucial relationships in 2 Timothy 2:2. He reminds Timothy of the upward mentoring relationship with a mentor (Paul), an outward relationship with a team of fellow apprentices, and a downward relationship with future mentees. When any part of this triad is missing, the process suffers.

...in order to become his image bearer

Christ was not ambiguous when it came to identifying his disciples. In the Gospel narratives, Jesus clearly describes the marks or qualities that should distinguish his disciples from those of other teachers. These qualifying traits are a good starting point to assess our discipleship, along with that of those we are trying to mentor.

I describe them as:
- Whole life transformation (Luke 6:40)
- Sacrificial allegiance (Luke 14:26)
- Faithful obedience (John 8:31-32)
- Servant love (John 13:34-35)
- Spiritual fruitfulness (John 15:8)

Author and business consultant Stephan Covey had solid advice when he said, "Begin with the end in mind."

For Reflection

1. Using the description of discipleship above, how might you help someone grow into becoming a disciple?

2. In which aspect of discipleship are you weakest? Who might help you develop it?

4

An Audience of One

Finally then, brethren, we request and exhort you in the Lord Jesus,
that as you received from us instruction as to how you ought to walk
and please God (just as you actually do walk),
that you excel still more (1Thess. 4:1).

Several years ago my wife, Mary, and I received tickets from friends to see the "Phantom of the Opera" in Kansas City. Our friends told us that they had received the tickets as a gift but could not attend. The musical was beginning to travel across the country after a long and successful run on Broadway. We were very excited to see it and decided to make it a special theater date night.

Unaware that the auditorium doors closed just before Showtime because of the dramatic opening scene, we arrived just in time for the usher to hurry us to our seats in the third balcony. To our surprise, when we got there, they were already occupied. Checking both sets of tickets, the usher told us that there was a problem and took us back to the main ticket booth for resolution.

Looking at our tickets, the friendly manager frowned, explaining that they were phony tickets. Fearing arrest, fines, and expulsion, I quickly related how we got the tickets third hand, explaining that our friends (and our source of the tickets) would never do such a thing. We must have appeared convincingly embarrassed because the manager turned from sober to supportive.

With time running out, she offered the only two seats left in the theater. Somewhat apologetically, she explained that they were "limited visibility" seats, but we could have them if we wanted. Assuming the seats were probably behind the lighting booth in the rafters, we accepted the offer. After a hurried thank you, our usher speed-walked us, not up but down, to our main floor seats: front row-left! We were amazed that only a small corner of the left stage was hidden from our view. Super upgrade!

At intermission, thinking that I would never be this close to the stage again, I decided to explore the orchestra pit rather than the refreshment bar. Located under the stage just a few feet from our seats, I casually wandered down into the "pit" to check it out.

Fortunately, since the musicians were on break, there was no one around to hear my lame reason for being there. My first impression upon entering the "pit's" mysterious world was how casually messy it was. But after looking around, I looked out. What most intrigued me was the view from the "pit." Sunken beneath the stage, the only thing the orchestra members could see was the bottom of the stage and the conductor's platform. During the play, musicians wouldn't see the audience with the house lights down, let alone the actors on the stage.

My first thought was, "How inconvenient." But on further reflection, it made sense. They didn't need to see the stage or the audience; they only needed to see the conductor. Only the conductor needed to see the stage, and the musicians only needed to see him. Their role was to keep one eye on their music and the other on the conductor. He would cue them when to start or stop, how loud or soft, and how fast or slow to play. They were not performing for the actors or the audience, only for the conductor. It was the conductor's job to please the actors, audience, and owners. It was the musician's job to please the conductor.

It struck me how similar discipleship is to the pit orchestra. The Conductor of the orchestra calls us to follow him. Each musician/follower has their part to play, blending in with all the other parts to create beautiful music. Sometimes our part is to play the melody, other times harmony, and often we are not playing but just counting, waiting to add our small contribution. Even though we cannot see what is happening on stage, we add our part, blending it with others, giving harmony, depth, and clarity to the drama taking place on stage.

As musicians, our concern should not be ticket volume, how many showed up for the performance, or even the amount of applause. Our role is pretty simple: play our part well for the approval of the Conductor.

My next question was more personal: For whom do I play? Am I playing for the crowd's applause, the actor's praise, other musicians, -- myself? Or am I playing for an audience of One?

Jesus set the example as he explained in John 8:29.

And He who sent Me is with Me; He has not left Me alone, for I always do the things that are pleasing to Him.

Paul picks up this theme in his letters to the early churches.

So we have not stopped praying for you since we first heard about you. We ask God to give you complete knowledge of His will and to give you spiritual wisdom and understanding. Then the way you live will always honor and please the Lord (Col 1:9-10).

For we speak as messengers approved by God to be entrusted with the Good News. Our purpose is to please God, not people. He alone examines the motives of our hearts (1Thess. 2:4 NLT).

Our discipleship journey takes us from "it's all about me" to "it's all about Him." It's a process of maturity, learning to shift the focus from ourselves to the One who created and called us. We began our apprenticeship with Christ with a strong bent toward self-fulfillment and narcissism, wanting our spiritual needs met and our brokenness healed. But as we experience his gracious provision in our new life of faith, we need to refocus our eyes on Christ and his purposes.

I think David's commitment to an audience of One is why God refers to him as a "man after my own heart." David had his share of failures, but since David set his heart on one Person and repented following his failures, he repeatedly experienced new beginnings in his deepening relationship with God. In the Psalms, David expressed it this way:

One thing I have asked from the LORD, that I shall seek: That I may dwell in the house of the LORD all the days of my life, To behold the beauty of the LORD And to meditate in His temple (Psa. 27:4).

As part of God's orchestra, our role is a gift. Whether we play oboe or violin, first chair or last, melody or harmony, we are to play our part with enthusiastic excellence--for the Conductor.

Some days I think I get it--some days not. Most days are a mixture of motives that are not clear. So I welcome Paul's prayer of Col 1:9-10 for spiritual wisdom and understanding. I need the Holy Spirit's work of liberation from my self-centeredness to "walk worthy of the Lord and please Him in all respects," performing my part for an audience of One.

For Reflection

1. What concepts or perspectives can help us make the shift from using God to pleasing Him?

2. Can you describe a time when the part God had you playing made you discontent?

5

The Fear Factor

That's the whole story.
Here now is my final conclusion:
Fear God and obey His commands,
for this is everyone's duty (Ecc. 12:13 NLT).

The Oldsmobile was an American automobile icon. First built in 1897, it sold more than 35 million automobiles over its 107-year history. During the 1980s, Olds tried to recapture its declining market by reinventing itself. In 1988 it came out with the slogan, "It's not your father's Oldsmobile." The company tried to reposition the elegant Olds as something different from what it was. It was the beginning of the end. The Oldsmobile was phased out in 2004.

Could it be that in an attempt to recapture a declining audience, the church has copied the Oldsmobile strategy by trying to reinvent God? Are we in danger of domesticating the Lion of Judah and emasculating the King of Kings?

Our culture certainly has lost the fear of the Lord. It is most often absent in Hollywood, schools, government, and many homes. It's not that God is absent, but we have turned God into whatever we want Him to be. He is a convenient icon to be made and used at our discretion. He is a P.S. to our history, an appendix to our essay, and only a conclusion to our speeches. The critical question for the church today is, "Have we corporately and individually lost the fear of God?"

The fear of God is not an outdated, primitive view held by unenlightened and superstitious people who were just too ignorant to know better. It is a theme that runs throughout Scripture from Genesis to Revelation. Moses taught it (Deuteronomy 10:12, 20-21); the Psalmist reflected on it (Psalm 103:13); Jesus stressed it (Matthew 10:28); Paul preached it (Philippians 2:12), and the early church got it (Acts 9:31). But to our shame and detriment, somewhere along the line, we have lost it.

What is the fear of God?

Fear is a broad term that can mean anything from fright and terror to reverence and veneration. We often use it to refer to our phobias, which run into the hundreds. New ones are discovered every day. Daily news and advertising continually prey on our fears, whether real or imaginary. At one time or another, we are given the impression that just about everything in our lives is a threat or unsafe. Hollywood feeds our fear with its love affair with disaster and end-of-the-world movies.

But fear is not always a bad thing. Actually, it is a gift from God. When our lives are threatened, we feel fear. Healthy fear moves us to take protective action. Fear also keeps us (most of us) from taking risks beyond our ability. Parents wisely keep close tabs on young children near cliffs because they know that the "fear factor" is not fully developed. (Someone also needs to keep tabs on senior men who climb ladders for the same reason!)

Some, like Timothy Treadwell, pay the ultimate price when they lose their healthy gift of fear. Mr. Treadwell lived among grizzly bears in Alaska for many years, assuming they were his friends. In 2003, Mr. Treadwell and his girlfriend were killed and eaten by the bears he no longer feared. Fear is a gift.

The term "fear of God" is not about feeling terror that causes us to shrink from his presence. Instead, it is a reverential fear described in Vine's Expository Dictionary of New Testament

Words as the "controlling motive of the life, in matters spiritual and moral, not a mere 'fear' of his power and righteous retribution, but a wholesome dread of displeasing Him." The reverential fear of God is based on his power and holiness, as revealed in Scripture, and should lead us to ask two questions. "How can we ever be right with God or live in his presence? And does our current gospel message of the love of God adequately reflect the fear of God?"

The good news is that when we come to God by grace through faith, the fear of condemnation is eliminated, so we no longer need to hide from his presence. Jesus Christ is now our high priest, making it possible to "draw near with confidence to the throne of grace, so that we may receive mercy and find grace to help in time of need" (Hebrews 4:16). Therefore, we can approach him confidently, but we should also approach him reverently with awe and gratitude. The reverent fear of God is the platform for our entire journey of faith.

The Bible presents God as both transcendent and immanent. God's transcendence refers to an aspect of his nature and power that is wholly independent of the material universe. It is the transcendence of God that forms the basis for awe, reverence, or fear. God's immanence (not to be confused with his imminence) refers to his presence everywhere within his creation. God is present in it but distinct from it. God's transcendence tells us God is above us; his immanence says he is close to us.

I wonder today if we have sacrificed God's transcendence for his immanence. One contributor to a loss of reverence is the changing style of worship. Many of our worship services promote entertainment and a casual "coffee house" atmosphere rather than a quiet reverence and awe before God. Maybe this is a reaction to the cold, formal worship of the past.

Cathedral architecture in medieval Europe put the focus on God's transcendence. Everything about those structures takes one's vision up. Spires, columns, even art were intended to stress the holiness, grandeur, and magnitude of God. Early cathedrals didn't even have pews in which to sit. You came and stood in the presence of a transcendent God. The relationship with God was vertical. It was also distant.

Compare that with today's church architecture. In most modern churches, if you look up, you see heating ducts, lights, and sound equipment – one look is enough. The result is the focus is more on the immanence of God, the horizontal. Even the theater-style seating forces one to look down versus up. The highest thing we look at is the video screen. This emphasis promotes the sense of God being with us more than above us, focusing on what is happening on the stage rather than in the heavens.

Since both God's transcendence and immanence are critical to knowing him, we need to find a way to keep both in perspective lest we error and fall off the cliff on either side. I wonder if today, in our desire to make God accessible, we have turned him into more of a rock star than the holy God of creation.

I wonder, too, how well we are teaching the fear of God to the next generation. I know there has been a strong reaction to previous generations that presented God as stern, angry, vengeful, and usually unapproachable. That view of God is not accurate either, but neither is the one that makes God our "buddy."

For Reflection

1. In what ways are we modeling an attitude of awe, reverence, and respect for God?

2. How might we teach the reverent wonder of God to the next generation?

6

Living the Wow

For Your unfailing love is higher than the heavens.
Your faithfulness reaches to the clouds (Psa. 108:4).

For God's family of faith, the fear of the Lord on the resurrection side of the cross means respect, reverence, wonder, and awe. It is the response of the soul to the majesty and glory of God that says, "Wow!"

Freed from the penalty of sin and transferred from the kingdom of darkness into the kingdom of light, our journey of discipleship is an invitation to explore the incredible majesty of God. Every day we should reflect on God and be amazed.

Rather than looking at God as a capricious cop or a demanding dictator, the fear of the Lord anticipates seeing something new, beautiful, and wonderful. The writer of Lamentations expressed it this way:

The faithful love of the LORD never ends! His mercies never cease. Great is His faithfulness; His mercies begin afresh each morning (Lam. 3:22-23 NLT).

The Apostle Peter takes the wow a step further in his second letter. He tells us that we are to diligently add to our faith qualities like knowledge, self-control, perseverance, and godliness (2 Peter 1:5+). The biblical concept of godliness has, at its root, the fear of God.

Godliness is described as "character and conduct determined by the principle of love and fear of God in the heart." [1] In earlier history it was called piety, which Webster defines as a "compound (combination) of veneration or reverence of the Supreme Being and love of his character, or veneration accompanied with love."[2]

In other words, godliness expresses reverence with holy living and affection/devotion. It is the response of the soul to the majesty and glory (wow) of God.

The implication from Peter's challenge is that the fear of the Lord can and must intentionally be developed. We are charged with its development along with other traits such as self-discipline and love. Peter makes it clear that far from being an elective, the fear of the Lord is critical to our journey of discipleship.

When understood and embraced, the fear of the Lord:

Turns knowledge into wisdom

- Marvels at both his works and ways.
- Celebrates our created dignity while retaining humility.
- Sees God's touch in life's ordinary events.
- Keeps a clear distinction between the Creator and his creation.

Accepts all of his revealed nature without distortion

- Prevents the love of God from trumping his holiness
- Keeps the Lion of Judah from becoming the genie of Aladdin
- Replaces embezzlement of his generous resources with stewardship
- Protects the transcendence of God from being diminished by his immanence.

Reverent wonder seeks to know God as he is rather than according to what we want him to be. However, too often, we want God to fit into our mental box so we can manipulate and control him. We tend to ignore or minimize the traits of God that threaten our contrived picture. The godliness and reverent wonder that Peter refers to seeks to know about him and please him. It results in an attitude of grateful love and constant devotion. It is a response that honors, respects, and responds to the will of God (John 17:4).

Moses is an example of a man who sought the reverent fear of God. Tasked with leading Israel to the Promised Land, Moses makes two requests of the Lord recorded in Exodus 33. "Now therefore, I pray You, if I have found favor in Your sight, let me know Your ways that I may know You" (Exod. 33:13). Later Moses said, "I pray You, show me Your glory" (Exod. 33:18)!

The first request was to know God's ways and the second to see God's glory. The mission before Moses was so humanly impossible that he felt the need to see the magnitude and splendor of God. When faced with challenges, both the unknown and the impossible, maybe we should borrow the lines from Moses' story, "Show me your ways and your glory."

When gripped by reverent wonder, it will be hard to defend our sinfulness or justify our self-centeredness. When the eyes of our soul see God revealed in power, greatness, love, compassion, and creative genius, we will not hesitate to lean into him as our source of strength and confidence.

If we want to gaze in reverent wonder at the nature of God, we have only to look at Jesus.

In the past God spoke to our forefathers through the prophets at many times and in various ways, but in these last days he has spoken to us by his Son, whom he appointed heir of all things, and through whom he made the universe. The Son is the radiance of God's glory and the exact representation of his being, sustaining all things by his powerful word (Hebrews 1:1-3).

Acts 22 records the Apostle Paul's confrontation with the risen Christ on the road to Damascus. Paul asked two questions, which we should ask every day if we are to grow in reverent wonder: "Who are you, Lord, and what do you want me to do?"

Here are several suggestions that I have found helpful to increase my reverent fear of the Lord:

- Reflect on all the defining moments in Christ's narrative.
- Reflect on God's fingerprint in his design of the cosmos at both the micro and macro levels.
- Reflect on the touch of God in the defining moments of your own life stories.
- Study the lives of biblical characters as they experienced God's loving-kindness, patience, discipline, judgment, wrath, and forgiveness, asking, "What does this story tell me about God?"
- Read about heroes of the faith, looking for how they experienced the touch of God.

[1] International Standard Bible Encyclopedia
[2] Webster dictionary 1828

For Reflection

1. What helps you reflect on God's reverent wonder?

2. What robs you of seeing God's majesty?

7

Highway Hazards

'For I know the plans that I have for you,' declares the LORD,
'plans for welfare and not for calamity
to give you a future and a hope' (Jer. 29:11).

Speedbumps, potholes, and detours are common hazards on almost every trip. We usually don't plan on them, but again, neither are we surprised when they show up. Each one is there for a different reason and has a unique way of altering our plans.

Speedbumps are not accidental but intentionally placed to slow traffic. They are usually in places where we need to be more attentive to our surroundings. Residential neighborhoods often install them to protect children, especially after discovering that speed limit signs are ineffective.

The inconvenience of speedbumps often irritates me. They slow me down and mess with my schedule. I usually question the city planners' sanity as I calculate how fast I can go over them without doing damage to my car.

Our spiritual journey also has speedbumps. Life's speedbumps slow us down and force us to pay attention to what is going on around us. In a culture in which fast is good and quicker is better, we are in danger of running over or through people instead of slowing down for them. When spiritual signs like "Reduce Speed Ahead" don't work, we need a few speedbumps. They force us to slow down, look around, and proceed with caution. That is good advice at any age.

I think Abigail was a speedbump for David's fast-paced passion for revenge (1 Sam. 25). Having been rebuffed by Nabal (a wealthy, stingy rancher), David sets out on a path of justice (revenge). Abigail, Nabal's wife, intercepts David, graciously challenging his thinking. She was a speedbump that allowed David to slow down, gain perspective, and alter his actions. He could have ignored the warning but only to his peril.

Faithful are the wounds (speedbumps) of a friend, but deceitful are the kisses of an enemy (Prov. 27:6).

Events, people, even circumstances, can act as speedbumps warning us to slow down and proceed with caution. If we have faith that God is directing our journey, speedbumps can be signs of his presence. Maybe we ignore the slow down warnings, but our loving Father creates speedbumps because he would prefer we get bounced in our seat than cause an accident.

Potholes, on the other hand, are not there to warn us but to damage us. Potholes can appear when we least expect them. In Missouri we should always expect them, but sometimes we don't see them until it's too late. Ignored potholes can do significant damage, especially if we are traveling at a high rate of speed. When I was learning to drive and hit a pothole, my dad would say, "Son, that's what your steering wheel is for." Wise drivers avoid potholes.

Potholes are like moral temptations. In the fifth century, St Augustine taught that evil is a distortion of good. As potholes are distortions of the roadway, so temptations are distortions of the truth. Giving in to temptation and hitting potholes in the road should be avoided by steering around them, not through them.

Paul's warning to Timothy was to "flee from youthful lusts" (2 Tim. 2:27). Don't pretend they are not there; don't ignore them; don't drive over them. If a road is notorious for potholes, find another route! Solomon wrote, "Enter not into the path of the wicked, and go not in the way of evil men. Avoid it, pass not by it, turn from it, and pass away" (Prov. 4:14-15). Unfortunately,

Solomon disregarded his own advice.

Detours are yet another travel hazard. Unlike speedbumps, detours can be a significant disruption to our plans. Speedbumps momentarily affect us, but detours can last a lifetime. Some detour signs explain the course change like "bridge out" or "sinkhole ahead," but often they don't. They force us to alter our plans, take a different road, and drive around on some inconvenient secondary road with no immediate explanation. It seems that there are three good reasons God puts up detour signs in our lives.

The first is to avoid major trouble ahead. In this case God, in his wisdom, does not give us a choice but sovereignly redirects our route to keep us safe. Rather than being annoyed, we would welcome the warning if we could see life from his perspective.

I remember a detour in my career path that, at the time, seemed senseless and unfair. Management made a decision I felt was sending me on a path to nowhere. Years later I became aware that there was a potential "bridge out" circumstance I could not see. God used the "unfair" decisions of people over me to create a detour for my safety.

Detours can also be beneficial by forcing us to see landscapes we would have missed. When we focus on "getting there" (whatever "there" is), freeways and interstates are the logical options. But there is so much we won't see from the interstate. Detours have a unique way of taking us places we would not have chosen to go, but showing us the scenery we would have missed. God's detours can be a way of saying, "Look around. There is something I want you to see. You have not been here before; don't miss it."

A third reason God sends us on detours is to redirect our plans. After graduating in the '70s with a degree in engineering, I went to work for Boeing Aircraft in Seattle. My interstate led from

Iowa to Washington. I prayed about it; I got the job; the interstate looked clear. I was on cruise control -- until I hit a "detour" sign. During the Viet Nam war period, the military draft took me off my freeway and into territory I would not have chosen.

There were other detours during that period that also caused me to hang on to God's promise in Proverbs 3:5-6: "Trust in the LORD with all your heart and do not lean (rely) on your own understanding. In all your ways acknowledge Him, And He will make your paths straight."

The verse does not say don't use your understanding, but rather don't rely on it. After several successive detours, my off-road route led me to a fulfilling career I had not seen from the freeway. The detour changed my compass heading and took me on a whole new adventure. Thank you, Father, for the uncomfortable detours that protect and guide.

On the resurrection side of the cross, we need to slow down for speedbumps, avoid potholes, and embrace detours.

For Reflection

1. Describe a time when a life speedbump made you slow down.

2. Think of a detour in your life that took you places you had not planned on. What did you see?

8

Real Life Monopoly

Set your mind on the things above,
not on the things that are on earth (Col. 3:2).

Board games may be going the way of the dinosaur, but Monopoly will always be the genre's icon. One version of the origin of the game goes something like this:

Living at the time of the Great Depression, Charles Darrow was jobless. Sitting around the family table at night with much time on his hands, he came up with an idea for a new family game. Cutting out a large cardboard square, Charlies lined the perimeter with names of streets connected to Atlantic City's Boardwalk. He then added some railroads, dice, buttons, and some hand-carved houses and hotels - along with the miracle bank that never ran out - and the game of Monopoly was born.

Since his neighborhood friends enjoyed playing it so much, Charles took his idea to Parker Brothers, hoping to sell it. After a corporate evaluation, they rejected it, saying it would never sell because it violated 52 guidelines for a good "family game," including it should not take more than 45 minutes to play and completed after one trip around the board.

Now, 90+ years later, with over 200 million copies sold worldwide, Monopoly is the most popular board game of the 20th century with multiple versions and advertising schemes.

Reflecting on the popularity of the game, I've pondered the reason behind its success. To the original generation, it was apparent. It offered a fun way to pass the time, it provided a dream of getting out of the depression, and there was little alternative recreation. A generation later, I grew up playing the game for the same reasons accept we had the cold war rather than the depression; we needed some entertainment to pass the long, dreary winters in Iowa. Our games could last for days, depending on how much real-life cheating and scheming went on.

But why has it been so popular in succeeding generations and even overseas? Then it hit me. It captured what we usually think of as success. Where else can you go and in a few hours (days), create a world where you can:

- Get rich
- Bankrupt your neighbor and
- Dominate the world?

Monopoly is an excellent metaphor for our natural life. In *Monopoly*, success is measured by how many possessions (money and property) we can acquire on our way to dominance. We have little concern for others or charitable giving unless we land on Community Chest. Round and round we go in the strategic pursuit of the "good life": accumulating wealth, avoiding jail, charging (and paying) rent. A life where the prevailing assumption is that success and happiness come from what we achieve and acquire.

Writing in the 5th century, St. Augustine recognized the world's "game of life" was the result of original sin, and the human desire to control, possess, and dominate, whether by ruling an empire or controlling a family. However, the gospel offers another way to live in this fallen, *Monopoly* world. It is the way to freedom: a transference from the kingdom of darkness to the kingdom of his Son (Col. 1:13). In his treatise, *The City of God*, Augustine saw the Christian faith as spiritually living in the City of God while physically residing in the city of the world. The former is primary and eternal and the later secondary and temporal.

Unfortunately, the Christian faith can function as a "get out of jail free" card acquired (when landing on "Chance") during one of our many trips around the board. We stash our "get out of hell free" card among our possessions with the plan to pull it out some future day when needed. Rather than our faith being a transfer from one kingdom to another, it is more like an addition to our current life. We may even add church and Bible study the way we would buy Baltic and Mediterranean – not much value but good to have in our portfolio. Our new Christianized *Monopoly* life goes on much the same as it always did. Our lives become syncretistic: a futile attempt to combine two opposing worldviews.

The Christian faith is not an "add on" but a transfer; designed to lift us out of our 2-dimensional, treadmill world into a 3-dimensional experience with Christ and his kingdom. The gospel presents a new reality through the lens of faith - more like a 3-D *Monopoly*! (Maybe someone will invent one; there is already a 3-D *Scrabble*!).

In our new kingdom of light, success is not measured by what we accomplish or possess, but whom we know! Contrary to the prevalent view that eternal life as a condo in heaven on a golf course, lake, or ocean, Jesus said eternal life is all about knowing him:

And this is eternal life that they may know Thee, the only true God, and Jesus Christ whom Thou hast sent (John 17:3).

In Matthew's record of the "Sermon on the Mount," Jesus gives a clear warning.

Not everyone who calls out to Me, 'Lord! Lord!' will enter the Kingdom of Heaven. Only those who actually do the will of My Father in heaven will enter. On judgment day many will say to Me, 'Lord! Lord! We prophesied in Your name and cast out demons in Your name and performed many miracles in Your name.'

But I will reply, 'I never knew you. Get away from Me, you who break God's laws' (Mat 7:21-23 NLT).

Our faith does not remove us from living in a Monopoly world, but it does free us from playing the game in the same way. It adds a new dimension of reality, intentionally developed through a lifestyle of apprenticeship/discipleship to Christ and his kingdom.

For Reflection

1. What other similarities does *Monopoly* have with living in the current world system?

2. How should adding a third spiritual dimension change how we live in a 2-D world? What does not change?

9

Flatland to Spaceland

*For the law of the Spirit of life in Christ Jesus
has set you free from the law of sin and of death* (Rom. 8:2).

On December 17, 1903, at Kitty Hawk, North Carolina, Orville and Wilbur Wright made history when they flew a heavier-than-air machine 120 feet (less than the wingspan of many modern aircraft). That event opened a new perspective that changed our lives forever. We were no longer confined to the surface of the earth under the control of gravity: we could fly. Space travel became a real possibility.

During the Enlightenment, pioneers like Newton and Bernoulli discovered another law: the law of lift. The new law of lift didn't eliminate the law of gravity, but it did counter it. This new law states that if air passes over a specific shape, an upward force results, causing the shape—and whatever is connected to it—to lift into the exciting space dimension. This law explains why gliders and jumbo jets fly, and rocks do not.

Life in a two-dimensional (2-D), natural world illustrates residing in our world without God. In the natural world, spiritual gravity (sin) not only holds us captive but distorts the beauty of the two dimensions. However, lift (the gospel or the Spirit of life in Christ) sets believers free from the limitations and penalty of gravity to live with a new spiritual dimension.

Paul explains this new freedom (a third dimension) in Romans 8:1-2, "Therefore, there is now no condemnation for those who are in Christ Jesus, because through Christ Jesus the law of the Spirit of life set you free from the law of sin and death."

More than one hundred years ago, Edwin Abbott wrote "Flatland," an allegory that shows how difficult it is to comprehend a new dimension. Flatland is a world of two-dimensional geometric shapes (picture living on the top of a table). There are length and width, but no height. Expressed through the eyes of Mr. Square, a very respectable gentleman, the allegory is about 2-D shapes like circles, lines, and triangles contentedly living in Flatland.

One day Mr. Square meets Mr. Sphere, who is from a three dimensional (3-D) world. In their curious conversation, Mr. Sphere insists that there are three dimensions, not just two. As a sphere, this character knows about length and width but also height. From his third dimension of height, Mr. Sphere explains that he can see "down," right into the homes of Flatlanders—something the square cannot fathom. Unaffected by Mr. Sphere's logic, he rejects the third dimension as even a possibility.

Out of frustration, Mr. Sphere lifts Mr. Square into the third dimension; now, he can look down. Shazam! He gets it. Mr. Square now understands up and down. The idea of height is added to length and width. The allegory continues as Mr. Square is placed back down into Flatland and tries in vain to explain his new experience to those still trapped in two dimensions.

Abbot wrote his book to attack the social structures of his day. However, when I read it years ago, Flatland helped me understand why our faith journey involves encountering the third, spiritual dimension. Jesus comes to us squares as a Sphere. And, like in Flatland, he not only describes life in the third dimension, he offers to lift us up and allow us to experience its reality. Then he begins a transformational process to fit us into this third dimension called the kingdom of God.

God originally designed humans as three dimensional—spiritual beings. But the 3-D experience was short-lived. As a result of the fall, we lost our spiritual dimension and became trapped in a two-dimensional natural world (Genesis 3). Yet the human heart still longs for this missing dimension as Solomon says, "He has set eternity in their heart" (Ecclesiastes 3:11). This vertical tug reminds us of what we lost. The gospel message of the kingdom is that we can be reborn and to recover this lost dimension. What Adam lost is now reestablished by the second Adam, Jesus Christ.

Some seek to escape Flatland by religion and self-effort. But this self-effort is like using a pogo stick to escape gravity. When I was growing up, the pogo stick was as popular as the skateboard is today. We jumped around like kangaroos trying to escape gravity, even if for only a few seconds—boing... boing... boing.

In the same way, religious self-effort offers short-lived attempts to escape our 2-D world. If we looked at our self-effort as God does, it would seem silly if not so tragic. Only the gospel and discipleship can supernaturally free us from the spiritual gravity limitations that trap us to life in Flatland. Jesus came announcing permanent freedom from our 2-D, natural world, and entrance into a new dimension: the kingdom of God.

For now, our spiritual third dimension influences but does not eliminate the other two dimensions. The challenging adventure of discipleship on the resurrection side of the cross is learning how to live in our natural world with our new spiritual dimension. We don't escape (yet) the pull of gravity, but we have freedom from its control.

Once having experienced the new spiritual dimension, our mission is to tell our fellow citizens in Flatland that there is an *up.*

Since you have been raised to new life with Christ, set your sights on the realities of heaven, where Christ sits in the place of honor at God's right hand. Think about the things of heaven, not the things of earth. For you died to this life, and your real life is hidden with Christ in God (Col. 3:1-3).

For Reflection

1. What makes living in all three dimensions difficult for you?

2. How do we make our new third dimension our primary/priority dimension?

10

Reducing the Tension in Discipleship

So then, my beloved, just as you have always obeyed,
not as in my presence only, but now much more in my absence,
work out your salvation with fear and trembling;
for it is God who is at work in you,
both to will and to work for His good pleasure (Phil. 2:12-13).

There are aspects of the Christian life that are paradoxical, causing tension when we can't resolve them. As a rule, we tend to polarize what we cannot harmonize, emphasizing one over the other, or promoting one at the other's expense. Church denominations have been built around this type of tension. Although some tension is unavoidable, we can also create tension by unnecessary polarization.

Remember the old question, "Did you walk to school or carry your lunch?" It's humorous because it proposes an unnecessary choice. You may need to choose between walking to school and riding your bike, but you don't need to choose between how you travel to school and what you have for lunch. You can easily do both. The tension is unnecessary.

An example of this kind of created tension in discipleship is the polarization of the concepts of grace and effort. Somewhere along our Christian journey, we heard the question, "Are you going to live by grace or effort?" Rather than considering it a humorous, irrelevant question, we think the two concepts are incompatible and mutually exclusive. We take it seriously and believe we need to choose between them. When we polarize two different ideas (e.g., belief and action), the tension is unnecessary and ultimately detrimental since both are biblical and essential to our discipleship journey.

Grace vs. effort is a polarization of attitudes (motives) vs. action (behavior). In our relationship with Christ, we need to understand that these two are not mutually exclusive. We certainly must choose whether we base our acceptance with God on his grace or our merit. We cannot do both simultaneously. However, effort is a behavior/action, not a motivation/attitude. If our effort (behavior) comes from a mindset of earning God's acceptance, then we need to change our perspective, not necessarily our actions.

A friend of mine was recently diagnosed with type 2 diabetes. He told me that it was a wakeup call as to how and why he ate. Before the diagnosis, he lived to eat. Now he eats to live. The diabetes solution was not to stop eating but to change his motivation behind eating. In our culture we tend to eat for entertainment and comfort – not real healthy reasons. The solution to a healthy diet is not to quit eating but to reprogram our minds about why and what we eat.

Effort is a significant theme in discipleship on the resurrection side of the cross. We are to work, train, do, put off, and put on. These actions are not competing with grace but are complementary to it. When we polarize them, we create unnecessary tension and destroy the dynamic partnership captured in Phil. 2:12-13.

So then, my beloved, just as you have always obeyed, not as in my presence only, but now much more in my absence, work out your salvation [effort]*with fear and trembling; for it is God who is at work in you* [grace motivation], *both to will* [attitude] *and to work [action] for His good pleasure.*

If we don't start with grace as the foundation for our acceptance with God, our effort (or work) can become a source of merit.

We need to understand at a heart level that God accepts us on the merits of Christ and not our own: grace. Grace based living is a counter-cultural reality that continually needs affirmation if we are to follow Christ on the resurrection side of the cross.

But having accepted the grace foundation, we need to work hard because our effort now serves a whole new purpose. The Apostle Paul frequently combines both grace and effort.

We proclaim Him, admonishing every man and teaching every man with all wisdom, so that we may present every man complete in Christ. For this purpose also I labor (effort), striving according to His power (grace), which mightily works within me (Col. 1:28-29).

Writing to the Corinthians about giving generously, Paul referred to this act as a "gracious work." He saw grace and work not as polar but complementary. If we are doing what Scripture commands, but with a wrong attitude, we need to change our perspective, not necessarily the actions. Grace is in tension with earning, not with effort. Scripture describes discipleship as a walk, run, race, even warfare, requiring diligence, discipline, and perseverance, all of which are sustained by the Holy Spirit's gracious power.

Living under grace is not passive. In the book of Galatians, written to emphasize that God's work of redemption is one of grace, ends with this exhortation:

Do not be deceived, God is not mocked; for whatever a man sows, this he will also reap...Let us not lose heart in doing good, for in due time we will reap if we do not grow weary (Gal 6:7-9).

A life lived under grace is one of serious sowing.

Along our discipleship journey, we may slip back into the default thinking of doing what is right to gain God's acceptance. It is a pattern that is not easy to break. At times we may think, for example, that by serving or memorizing Scripture, or obeying a command that God now owes us some answers to prayer or maybe a little credit next time we slip up. When this happens, we need to review our grace foundation, remind ourselves of who we are in Christ, and why; then we can re-engage in working out our salvation but from a different motivation.

For Reflection

1. What other spiritual truths do you find challenging to harmonize?

2. What are other spiritual truths we tend to polarize?

11

The Day the Music Died

Sing to Him a new song;
Play skillfully with a shout of joy (Psa. 33:3).

Imagine an old, broken piano, maybe one you've seen in an old barn. The keys are yellow with age; some are missing leaving significant gaps in the keyboard. The piano bench is on its side with a broken leg. You look inside to see the soundboard cracked and broken. Most of the strings are either missing, broken or not connected. Noticing the manufacturer's name, you know that it was a beautiful instrument at one time.

Hold that picture in the back of your mind as you read on.

"The day the music died" is a memorable line from the iconic 1971 lament, "American Pie" by Don McLean. The song reflects the changes that happened through the turbulent 60s, beginning with the death in 1959 of rock and roll star Buddy Holly.

The eight and a half minute long "song of the century" created an endless discussion about the meaning of the various verses. Asked what the lyrics of "American Pie" really meant, McLean replied, "It means I never have to work again!"

In the song, McLean captures more than he intended with the phrase "the day the music died." Our real lament is not for the lost days of rock and roll, Bobby Dylan, the Beatles, or the simplicity of a previous decade but rather for the loss of the song God designed us to play. The Bible tells us we lost our real Song in the Garden when the piano on which it was played lost its strings, and the music died.

Solomon reminds us that although we have lost the Song, there is still a faint echo of the melody residing in the heart of every man and woman. "He also has set eternity in their heart" (Ecc. 3:11).

The Psalmist said, "He put a new song in my mouth, a song of praise to our God; Many will see and fear And will trust in the LORD" (Psa. 40:3). The book of Revelation repeats the idea, "And they sang a new song saying, "Worthy are You to take the book and to break its seals" (Rev. 5:9).

However, to be heard, God's Song needs an instrument. Returning to your image of the old piano, picture that piano as who you once were. But through the gospel of Christ, your soundboard has been replaced, and you have been given new strings. The great piano Restorer is renewing the outside and slowly replacing the keys. With each new key, the sound gets better. And now the Restorer asks you to play his song.

Even if given a Steinway, a person should not expect to play music without training his mind and body to master the skills of a pianist. Simply telling people how great the music is, how others long to hear it, and how well it is composed does not equip a person to play it on his piano.

Without training and practice, we can play notes but not real music. Discipleship is the process of learning to play God's music on our refurbished pianos. He has given us the song to play, but we need to understand the fundamentals of music, the names of notes, and their location on the keyboard. If we do not possess the skills to play, we can make noise but not music.

In Meredith Wilson's 1957 classic musical, "The Music Man," Professor Hill, masquerading as a traveling band instructor, cons the citizens of River City. He promises them that they can keep their boys out of trouble by creating a real marching band. All they need to do is buy all the equipment from him, including instruments, uniforms, and music. Once the equipment arrives (and he has his money), he plans to skip town. When forced to explain how they are to play music with their instruments, Hill tells the boys to use the "Think System," in which they have to only think of a tune over and over, and they will know how to play it without ever practicing on their instruments.

It seems that Professor Hill has slipped into our Christian communities and convinced us that we, too, can play spiritual music with just the "Think System." All we need to do is think about it, and we will play the Song.

I am afraid that much of our Christian ministry leaves people standing on the train station platform as Professor Hill leaves town. They are all decked out in their uniforms and proudly holding their instruments but still wondering how to play. As he fades from sight, they shout in unison, "So how do we play the music?" He yells back, "Just use the Think System!" Then, most go home and put their instruments away.

Intention is no substitute for action.

Another common trend is to substitute music appreciation for music proficiency. We promote skilled musicians, putting them on stage where people come to enjoy their performance. People then go from one concert to another, appreciating the music but not learning to play it. Rather than the concert being catalytic for inspiring new musicians, it becomes a substitute for learning to play.

We should listen to great musicians and appreciate their music, but we should also learn to play our own instruments. As our children were growing up, they were required to play some instrument. They all started on the piano and then moved to an instrument of their choice: flute, violin, and trombone. Because they were learning to play themselves, "professional" musicians were motivating, not as a substitute but as an example.

After teaching beginning piano for 20+ years, my wife observed a critical difference between those who quit and those who learned to play music. Proficiency was more about discipline than ability. By practicing, many of the students who lacked natural talent learned to play well and enjoy it. Those who quit wanted to play music, but they didn't want to expend the effort to learn how and eventually lost interest altogether.

A few people learn on their own and "play by ear," but they are the exceptions. I had an uncle who could hear a melody and then sit down at the piano and play it, never having had a lesson in his life. No one else in the family got the gene. The rest of us learn to play through training and practice: one note, one line, one page at a time.

The music has not died. God gives the Song and renews our broken instruments, but we need to learn, practice, and keep our instruments in tune. Most of us also need some personal coaching to become accomplished spiritual musicians; that is called discipleship. Those equipped to come alongside aspiring spiritual musicians and take them to a higher level are disciple-makers.

For Reflection

1. Think of a time when a particular practice/discipline became a delight rather than a duty.

2. What are the benefits when practice is no longer a duty or just a discipline?

12

The Gospel of the Gaps

Remember that you were at that time separate from Christ,
excluded from the commonwealth of Israel,
and strangers to the covenants of promise,
having no hope and without God in the world (Eph. 2:12).

The term "God of the gaps" was first used in the 19th century, referring to a theological argument in which God is the reason for any phenomenon that couldn't be explained by the current scientific understanding. But a form of "God of the gaps" has been around for a long time. Pagan religions throughout history believed there must be a god or gods who controlled what they could not – which was almost everything. Therefore, people needed a god of the harvest, fertility, war, disease, and love to give hope. Pagan worship was built around placating or bribing the gods to intervene for the benefit of the worshipper. If things went well, the gods were pleased. If they went poorly, the gods were angry.

With the Enlightenment period of European history, man gradually gained increased knowledge and control over his life and environment. The result was the inevitable decreasing need for a belief in a God of the gaps. Postmodern man considers medieval religious beliefs mythical, unnecessary--even silly. Compared to our early ancestors, the self-sufficient modern man admits to few things being outside his control. Why pray to a god of war when you can build a bigger bomb?

However, today the pagan God of the gaps idea is just below the surface. Consider what happened right after "911". For the following several months, churches experienced a surge in attendance. Public conversation, which generally avoided any mention of God or prayer, was temporarily filled with it. The vulnerability of the moment led to a revival of the "God of the gaps." The standard politically correct view of avoiding any mention of God was then, and is still today, temporarily suspended during national or natural tragedies.

But closer to home in our evangelical world, I wonder if we haven't exchanged a "god of the gaps" for a "gospel of the gaps." Early in my evangelism training, I learned a strategy called "open nerve" evangelism. The rationale is that not everyone has a felt gap of sin, but they do have overwhelming issues such as loneliness, grief, lack of direction, anger, or any host of other felt needs. According to the gospel of the gaps, we need to identify those issues and show them how Christ can help. The unintended consequence is a presentation of God as the "Gap Filler."

Four of the more common significant gaps are:

1. The guilt gap: the need for freedom from the guilt of past and future sin.

2. The fear gap: the need for security over the unknown.

3. The eternity gap: the need for a guaranteed heavenly bliss.

4. The fulfillment gap: the need for a personal gift package to make our lives abundant.

We intend to later add, "Oh, by the way, now that you have come to Jesus, he wants you to follow him, take up your cross, daily die to yourself, serve others, and do everything for his glory." Naively we expected people to replace the "It's all about me" view of the gospel with "It's all about him." Some do. Most do not.

The problem with the gap message is not that it is untrue, but that it is inadequate. Wanting God to fill our gaps is not wanting too much but too little. It is undoubtedly true that Christ is interested in meeting our needs: healing our diseases, breaking chains of bondage, giving us peace, even restoring our fractured and fragile self-image. But the gospel Jesus taught, and Paul preached, was not a gospel of self-actualization or self-fulfillment. It was a gospel of the truth about God expressed through his Son. The good news that comes from the gospel is not about making our self-centered lives more self-oriented but about the freedom to join him in his kingdom life -- the reality for which we are designed and without which we are incomplete.

Nothing has changed in human nature in two thousand years. The people Jesus ministered to were more than willing to have him fill their gaps. They wanted his free meals, healing, and deliverance from oppression. What they rejected were the King and his kingdom.

A cursory study of the book of Acts and the gospel message taken from Jerusalem to the edges of the Roman world reveals a message of Christ and life in his kingdom. There was no promise of self-actualization or a more comfortable lifestyle, only a promise of freedom to know Christ and live with him in his kingdom kind of life.

For example, after explaining that the believers were not drunk at Pentecost, Peter tells the narrative of Jesus ending with Christ's exaltation at the right hand of God. His summary statement was: "Therefore, let all the house of Israel know for certain that God has made Him both Lord and Christ—this Jesus whom you crucified" (Acts 2:36).

When Paul introduces the gospel of Christ to the men of Athens on Mars Hill (Acts 17), he starts with God as the Creator and Lord of all creation. After claiming God's sovereignty over humanity and nations, he moves to a call for repentance in light of the One resurrected from the dead and who will judge the world. His gospel message was a little different from "God loves you and has a wonderful plan for your life." I wonder if Paul had the chance to speak today on our university campuses or Capitol Hill, would he say the same thing?

The gospel's early proclamation dealt with a God of the gap—not gaps; it was a relational and kingdom gap. "For he has rescued us from the kingdom of darkness and transferred us into the Kingdom of his dear Son, who purchased our freedom and forgave our sins" (Col 1:13-14).

For Reflection

1. What examples of the "God of the gaps" theory do you see in our culture?

2. What impact does a "gospel of the gaps" have on discipleship?

13

Unintended Consequences

Guard, through the Holy Spirit who dwells in us,
the treasure which has been entrusted to you (2 Tim. 1:14 NLT).

Honey, I Shrunk the Kids was a 1989 American family science fiction film produced by Walt Disney Pictures. It tells the story of an inventor who accidentally shrinks his and his neighbor's kids to a quarter of an inch with his electromagnetic shrinking machine. It is a whimsical adventure built around the law of unintended consequences.

Today I believe we are experiencing the unintended consequences of "shrinking" the gospel message as evidenced by the disparity between the everyday Christian life presented in the New Testament and what is being demonstrated in our culture today. Polls consistently reflect that a high percentage of Americans claim to be "born again" but show little statistical difference in values, morals, and behavior from those who don't. The lack of kingdom distinctive has become the new normal.

One cause is the lack of spiritual training and discipleship, but I wonder if there is a more systemic issue. I wonder if the epidemic of spiritual complacency regarding living a kingdom lifestyle goes back to our concept and presentation of the gospel message.

The term "gospel" means "good news," but good news about what? The word "gospel" is a headline in search of a story (content). There are many gospels out there, but what is the gospel that has the power of God for salvation, requiring faith and setting us free to live the eternal kind of life found in his kingdom?

When the New Testament writers use the term gospel, they usually follow it with a prepositional phrase "gospel of ___" which implies content (a story). The most common phrase is some variation of the words "Jesus Christ, the Lord."

The book of Romans is the most complete presentation of the gospel in the New Testament. In his introduction, Paul claims that he is an apostle set apart for the gospel. But what gospel?

Paul, a bond-servant of Christ Jesus, called as an apostle, set apart for the gospel of God...concerning His Son... Jesus Christ our Lord (Rom 1:1-3).

Paul continues in verse 16, "I am not ashamed of the gospel of Christ, for it is the power of God unto salvation" (KJV). The gospel Paul proclaims has the power to "save." It is the good news that has a specific outcome.

In Paul's introduction, he identifies the gospel from the general to the specific. It is first of all the "gospel of God." Then, to be more specific, it is "concerning his Son." Finally, to focus on who the Son of God is, Paul identifies him as "Jesus Christ our Lord."

Each of these names carries an aspect of the gospel message.

Jesus: The incarnate Son of God, a real flesh and blood person in the lineage of David

Christ: The anointed Deliverer, the One to bring redemption to a broken world

The Lord: The final Authority, King, Master, Ruler

The New Testament gospel is the good news about the Son of God, called Jesus, the Christ, the Lord: The One who makes life in his kingdom accessible. The gospel is about him. It is more than a doctrine; it is His Story--the whole story. The statement "God loves you and has a wonderful plan for your life," while true, is not the gospel. It gives a reason for and a result of the gospel, but it is not the gospel.

The first four books of the New Testament are called Gospels; each gives a portrait of the incarnate Son of God. Together they present a composite picture of who he is from before creation to the final judgment.

In his book, *Darwin's Black Box*, Michael Behe (biochemical researcher and professor at Lehigh University in Pennsylvania) introduced the concept he calls "irreducible complexity." In simple terms, this idea applies to any system of interacting parts in which the removal of any one part destroys the functionality of the entire system. An irreducibly complex system requires every component to be in place before it will function. The mousetrap is a simple example of irreducible complexity.

The mousetrap has five working parts, each of which must be present for the system to work at all. If you remove one part, the whole mechanism is inoperable.

So what is the "irreducible complexity" of the gospel?

If the gospel is the good news about Jesus, the Son of God, what about Jesus do we need to present (or believe) for the gospel to have power? Could it be that in our attempt to make the gospel marketable and simple in a soundbite world, we have actually "shrunk" it beyond its critical complexity, resulting in unintentional consequences?

What about Christ's narrative is optional to know, believe, or present? In the familiar John 3:16 passage, what is the "in him" that we are to believe? Most of us would quickly react to a "liberal" gospel that presents Jesus as merely a good teacher. However, what about a gospel that presents him as a good teacher and the sacrifice for sin? Is that enough? Is that all that needs to be believed?

The gospel of Christ on the resurrection side of the cross is a composite of all that is true about him from Creator to the final Judge. When we shrink the gospel message to only a few concepts (the cross and resurrection), as critical as they are, we create a dichotomy between evangelism and discipleship: an unintended consequence where discipleship becomes an elective and kingdom living an option.

For Reflection

1. In light of the current cultural drift from a Judaic/Christian worldview, what effect should it have on how we present the gospel of Christ?

2. If people don't know the Bible narrative's primary storyline, where should we start in explaining the gospel?

14

Now Playing: His Story

Him we proclaim,
warning everyone and teaching everyone with all wisdom,
that we may present everyone mature in Christ (Col. 1:28 ESV).

The gospel is a story: a drama of epic proportions. It is the revelation of God in and through his Son, the One we call Jesus, the Christ, the Lord (Romans 1:1-3). It is His Story. What may surprise us in this drama is that we are not the main characters or even the primary audience.

Look at how the Apostle Paul zooms out and looks at His Story from a cosmic perspective.

I was chosen to explain to everyone this mysterious plan that God, the Creator of all things, had kept secret from the beginning. God's purpose in all this was to use the church to display His wisdom in its rich variety to all the unseen rulers and authorities in the heavenly places. This was His eternal plan, which He carried out through Christ Jesus our Lord (Eph. 3:9-11 NLT).

Paul sees that the purpose of this great drama, the narrative of Jesus, is about revealing the manifold wisdom of God to a heavenly audience. The invisible (but real) spirit world is the audience, watching what is being played out on planet earth and observing with increased wonder of God's wisdom and glory. The one part of his creation made in his image is the supporting cast! We are being used to display his nature in all of its dimensions.

In our broken and sin infected world, we are how God displays the depth of his glory and wisdom. The angelic world is watching in amazement, and we, for a brief moment in time, get to experience it. It is not about us, but it is through us.

It may be humbling to realize that we are not the focus of this great drama. We are in the play to illuminate the incredible nature of the Author and Director of the Story. This concept is counter to our current narcissism in which our mantra is, "It's all about me." This defiant chant has echoed down the halls of history to the present day. The Bible begins the Story with the tragic fall of humanity into the "it's all about me" declaration. The hope of the Christian faith is its ability to deliver us from self-orientation slavery and isolation to realignment with Christ under his loving authority.

Now playing: *His Story.*

From the theater of heaven, the angelic audience is looking at a small but unique planet in a vast cosmos. With humanity on it, this planet is the central stage for the continued revelation of the vast wisdom of God.

Reading the introduction to the program for this cosmic drama, we discover:

- It is written and directed by God the Father
- The music is performed by the Holy Spirit
- The central character with the starring role is the Son of God, the second person of the Trinity
- The setting and background is the created cosmos
- Earth is the center stage: a significant, pale blue planet in the vast sea of the universe
- Supporting cast: All of humanity and in particular, those called God's family of faith

Time is described as either linear (*chronos*) or as a special moment (*kairos*). A *kairos* moment is not measured in hours, days, or years but as a period/season where something significant happens. It could happen in a few seconds or over a lifetime. The unfolding drama consists of seven defining (kairos) moments (Acts) in the narrative of the Son of God.

His Story reveals who he is, what he has done, what he is doing, and what he will do. Some of these moments are relatively short (*chronos* time), while others happen over long periods of history. In each of these kairos moments, God is revealed in Christ from a different viewpoint, with different names, allowing us to experience his multi-dimensional nature. Although he is always the same and never changes, his character becomes more evident with each defining moment, giving us a complimentary picture of the Son of God that together forms a grand, composite portrait.

The three names most associated with the Son of God can summarize His Story: Jesus + Christ + Lord. From Acts through Jude, the New Testament writers use this composite 85 times in various arrangements.

The name "Jesus" is mostly associated with his earthly life from his incarnation through his ascension. It is in the name Jesus that we most clearly get the concept that God has taken on flesh and blood, taken on our likeness.

Though He was God, He did not think of equality with God as something to cling to. Instead, He gave up His divine privileges; He took the humble position of a slave and was born as a human being (Phil. 2:6-7).

The name Jesus or Joshua was a common Hebrew name that meant savior. Although there was a prophetic meaning given by the angel to Mary (Matt 1:21), the name designated the man from Nazareth in Galilee, Joseph and Mary's son, the man who became a great rabbi. God could have selected it not only for its spiritual implication but for its ordinariness: The One who lived among us. The name Jesus summarizes the gospel's initial storyline: God now lives among us in the person of Jesus of Nazareth.

The name Christ adds more to His Story. Christ, the anointed One, the Messiah, brings the Old Testament expectation of a Deliverer, a Restorer of Israel, into the picture. From the crucifixion to the ascension, his story's defining moments are captured in Christ's names. The name Christ or Jesus Christ was a widespread way to refer to the Son of God on the resurrection side of the cross and summarized his role as Savior, Deliverer, and final High Priest.

The name Lord (although present in the Gospels) was amplified at his ascension when he takes his place at the right hand of God. Without the Son of God as Lord, the gospel is incomplete. It is as much a part of *His Story* as his crucifixion and resurrection.

From the beginning to the end of the book of Acts, those who carried the gospel told the story of the Son of God: Jesus Christ the Lord.

For Reflection

1. How does thinking of the gospel as his complete story impact discipleship?

2. How could thinking of the gospel as *His Story* affect our understanding of evangelism?

15

The Incarnation

And the Word became flesh, and dwelt among us,
and we saw His glory,
glory as of the only begotten from the Father,
full of grace and truth (John 1:14).

His Story: Prologue

Looking through the lens of the gospel, the Old Testament is
the backstory for this epic drama. Creation, the conflict between God and Satan, the Garden of Eden, the Patriarchs, and
the nation of Israel all serve as background to this unfolding
drama.

In the prologue, the second person of the Trinity (the Son of
God) is revealed as:

- **The agent of creation.**

*God, after He spoke long ago to the fathers in the prophets in
many portions and in many ways, in these last days has spoken
to us in His Son, ..., through whom also He made the world* (Heb.
1:1-2).

*For by Him all things were created, both in the heavens and on
earth, visible and invisible, whether thrones or dominions or rulers or authorities--all things have been created through Him and
for Him* (Col 1:16).

- **The Eternal Word**

In the beginning was the Word, and the Word was with God, and the Word was God. He was in the beginning with God. All things came into being through Him, and apart from Him nothing came into being that has come into being (John 1:1-3). (Also see Eph. 1:16-18)

During the prologue to His Story, speech brought forth a cosmos, new dimensions come into existence, matter is created, space is established, time begins, his likeness finds expression in humanity, and his glory is illuminated. But an attempt was made to hijack the story and set up humanity in the primary role and relegate the Creator to a supporting part.

A resistance movement now runs as a separate thread throughout the storyline. However, the Director weaves the conflict and broken relationships into a grander story of his grace and mercy. He folds the resulting pain and suffering into the storyline and uses it for his ultimate aim.

Although the plan is sabotaged and the design distorted, God begins a restoration process. A select group of people is chosen, his nature is revealed, his jealousy is experienced, heaven is illustrated in worship, his morality is explained in the Law, his holiness is expressed through the sacrifices, and his lineage is established for a coming Redeemer/King.

The Incarnation (Act 1)

It takes four millenniums for God to prepare the stage for the advent of his Son. But now it begins.

As the curtain pulls back, the angelic audience witnesses the eternal Son of God taking on humanity through an ordinary peasant girl in an obscure little hamlet called Bethlehem. They must have looked in wonder at this incredible display of God's humility: deity taking on humanity, eternity taking on time. On the stage, only a few people notice, just a few blue-collar shepherds, a small band of curious scientists, and one irate, paranoid king.

Years later, in the Apostle John's version of *His Story*, he begins with this defining moment. "And the Word became flesh, and dwelt among us, and we saw His glory, glory as of the only begotten from the Father, full of grace and truth" (John 1:14). The Apostle Paul commenting on Act 1, writes, "For in Christ lives all the fullness of God in a human body" (Col 2:9).

The angelic audience must have been amazed as they witness eternity becoming an embryo, glory hiding in the shadows, perfection becoming vulnerable, greatness disguised by the ordinary, and infinity clothed in mortality.

God, after He spoke long ago to the fathers in the prophets in many portions and in many ways, in these last days has spoken to us in His Son ... He is the radiance of His glory and the exact representation of His nature (Heb. 1:1-3).

It was a birth without parallel. More than a miraculous conception, it was a virgin conception, contrary to the laws of nature. his birth was not his beginning, but it was the beginning of the one we call Jesus.

The Son of God now calls himself the Son of Man, but his common, given name, is Jesus. Jesus is the English version of the Hebrew name *Yeshua* (a common name related to Joshua), which means salvation. Whenever this name appears, it should remind us that the eternal God took on human form and became one with us, fully human except for sin.

Jesus was aware of both this beginning and his eternal existence. "I came forth from the Father and have come into the world; I am leaving the world again and going to the Father" (John 16:28).

It remains a mystery how one person could be both fully God and fully man. The early church fathers expressed the tension of this conundrum at the Council of Chalcedon (451 A.D.), claiming that Jesus is "recognized in two natures [God and man], without confusion, without change, without division, without separation … not as parted or separated into two persons but one and the same Son and Only-begotten God the Word, Lord Jesus Christ."

As this Act ends, the star disappears, the magi sneak out of the country, the shepherds return to their mundane sheep, the tyrannical king lashes out, and Mary, Joseph, and the infant Jesus escape over the desert to live in exile. For the next 30 years, the world goes on much as it was -- but not for much longer.

For Reflection

1. What are some other implications of the incarnation?

2. What are the elements of a classic drama/story? How do they compare with *His Story*?

16

The Demonstration

For even the Son of Man did not come to be served,
but to serve,
and to give His life a ransom for many (Mark 10:45).

In Act 2 of our drama (*The Demonstration*), the Son of God, now called Jesus, is revealed as the Suffering Servant portrayed by Isaiah the prophet hundreds of years earlier. The heavenly audience sits in quiet amazement as they watch the prophecy take on reality.

The Creator of the universe, the One who spoke the entire universe into existence, lives in obscurity and works as a peasant and common laborer. They watch him get tired, hungry, sweaty, and blistered. But the hardest to watch is the mistreatment, rejection, and animosity by the very people he came to help.

Reflecting on this scene years later, the Apostle Paul writes, "Who, although He existed in the form of God, did not regard equality with God a thing to be grasped, but emptied Himself, taking the form of a bond-servant" (Phil 2:6-7). The Creator now serves the created.

Throughout this Act, truth walks in a body, light enters darkness, mystery takes on clarity, and power takes on poverty. For thirty-some years, omnipresence takes on space, omnipotence gets tired, and grace walks in sandals. The angelic audience sits amazed, wondering when Jesus will finally unleash his power, reveal his identity, and vindicate his glory. How long will this humiliation go on?

There are hints of his real power displayed in the context of daily life. He touches the blind and they see. He speaks and the demons retreat. He takes a small lunch, blesses it, and feeds thousands. He teaches and people's hearts stir. His presence is both attractive and threatening. He lifts up the discouraged and puts down the arrogant. He claims authority over the sacred Hebrew Scripture and yet commits himself to fulfill its prophecies. He is focused, yet never in a hurry. People he encounters are amazed, confused, excited, angry, loyal, and apprehensive.

Jesus lives out his humble life teaching and serving, but that is just what is happening on the surface. Outwardly he is our example, but at a deeper level, he is our substitute. His claim, both publically and privately, is that his real mission is to do the will of his Father. He claims that he only can do what he sees the Father doing. During his hidden and public years, Jesus, the Son of Man, lives in total alignment with his Father's will, as the first Adam should have.

So also it is written, "The first MAN, Adam, BECAME A LIVING SOUL." The last Adam became a life-giving spirit (1Cor. 15:45).

He lived as the second Adam in the way the first Adam should have. His total obedience to the Father's will gave him the right to represent all of humanity, becoming the substitute for our rebellion.

His life demonstrated not just alignment with God's moral code but submission to his will. In the victorious struggle played out in the Garden of Gethsemane, we catch a glimpse of the second Adam submitting to the will of the Father, saying, "Father, if You are willing, remove this cup from Me; yet not My will, but Yours be done" (Luke 22:42).

Earlier Jesus declared, "But so that the world may know that I love the Father, I do exactly as the Father commanded Me (John 14:31). "I glorified You on the earth, having accomplished the work which You have given Me to do" (John 17:4).

His sinless life qualified him to be the perfect Lamb of God who takes away the sin of the world. "He made Him who knew no sin to be sin on our behalf, so that we might become the righteousness of God in Him" (2 Cor. 5:21).

The Old Testament sets the standard for the acceptable sin sacrifice. In Israel's redemption story leaving Egypt, God required the people to spread the blood from a perfect lamb over their doorposts (Exodus 12:5). The tabernacle worship established by God through Moses, required various kinds of sacrifices.

One of the most critical was the annual sin offering. Once a year, the high priest would take the blood from an unblemished lamb and enter into the Holy of Holies, offering it for the people's sins. It was with this picture in mind that John the Baptist introduced Jesus as the Lamb of God.

During his short 30 plus years on planet earth, Jesus never traveled far from his home town. He spent most of his time among the poor and ordinary people of a small but contentious nation: a P.S. in the grand Roman Empire. He never wrote a book and trying, for the most part, to stay out of the view of the politicians and religious elite. He mostly taught about the arrival of the kingdom of God and about life in that kingdom. His message was as counter-cultural then as it is now, received with curiosity and skepticism. Yet he boldly claimed that his kingdom was now real and accessible. He is the only doorway to it and the rightful ruler of it.

The crowds, initially curious, even amazed at his teaching authority, took every opportunity to have him heal their sick, cast out their demons, and serve them a free meal. They hoped that he would eventually use his power to liberate their nation from the oppression of Rome, giving them the peace that has been so elusive. They were willing to promote him from a rabbi to a king if only he would do it now. However, as it became frustratingly apparent that a physical kingdom was not his plan, they turned on him, accusing him of made-up crimes and charges.

The angelic audience watches with increased anxiety as this Act goes from bad to worse; the storm clouds gather. The audience realizes that if his strategy is to gain a broad market for his message, it isn't working; opposition is escalating. The religious rulers, set on getting rid of him, have heard enough. The few friends and followers he has are scared, confused, and unpredictable. Then just when it seems like events couldn't get worse, they do.

For Reflection

1. What do you think is the popular view of Jesus as a man? How would He be described?

2. Why do you think the crowd made such a drastic shift from "Hosanna" one day to "crucify Him" the next?

17

The Crucifixion

But we preach Christ crucified,
to Jews a stumbling block and to Gentiles foolishness
(1Cor. 1:23).

Our next Act (The Crucifixion) lasts only a few days. However, the impact of this defining moment will be felt at a cosmic level forever. In the natural 2-dimensional world, an obscure rabbi is unjustly accused and murdered for religious blasphemy.

Maybe a big deal to a small religious sect at a brief moment in time, but certainly not something that would be remembered very long or change the direction of history. History makers are the Caesars, the Alexander the Greats, but certainly not this obscure rabbi they call Jesus.

Determined to eliminate the radical Rabbi Jesus, the Jewish leaders took their case to the Roman prefect. In the old days, they would have stoned him for their claim of his blasphemy, but Rome had taken away their right to capital punishment. Now they had to make a case severe enough to convince Pilate, the Roman governor, that it was in Rome's best interest to kill this popular teacher.

Their claim that he was a wayward rabbi didn't convince Pilate that he deserved the death penalty, so they switched their strategy to highlight Jesus's claim to be the king of a new kingdom. That did it. Now Pilot is listening. A possible insurrection around a popular figure who shifts from a religious zealot to a political threat got traction. Over his (and his wife's) better judgment, he caves in to the plot of capital murder.

After a mock trial and a severe beating, they crucified Jesus on a cross outside Jerusalem. By all rights, this should finish the story. He lived; he died; the end. As they put his body in a borrowed tomb, even his friends felt disappointment at the death of their dream: their hope sealed in a tomb. Three years of optimism crushed in one convincing stroke of Roman power.

It was a good ride as long as it lasted. Jesus certainly was a refreshing teacher. His interpretation (yoke) of the Old Testament brought new freedom from the Pharisees' insane legalism. He certainly did many acts of kindness and told stories worth remembering. His power over nature and the demonic world hinted that God still cared. Maybe he will be remembered as a benevolent teacher whose life is worth emulating, but his words of victory are forgotten for the moment.

However, on a higher, spiritual dimension, this defining moment was the laser point of God's masterplan: the fulfillment of a strategy laid out in the Trinity's eternal mind before forming the earth. The Son of God becomes Jesus, the Son of Man, who then becomes the Savior of the world. The accumulative sin of humanity is now placed on the innocent, perfect Lamb of God.

Reflecting on this scene a few years later, Paul said, "But God demonstrates His own love toward us, in that while we were yet sinners, Christ died for us" (Rom 5:8).

The ultimate "coup" is pulled off, rebellion is contained, the final sacrifice is made, sin is consolidated, God's wrath is expiated, and the Trinity experiences separation for the first time. At the cross, God's love meets his holiness in a brilliant display of grace. Creation is liberated from the curse of sin, and the bruised heel has finally crushed Satan's head (Gen. 3:15).

In a cruel event that would be a stumbling block to the Jews and foolishness to the Gentiles, God defeats Satan and redeems humanity. Satan didn't see it coming. He thought he had Jesus right where he wanted him. That's what he (Jesus) gets for turning down my offer of all the kingdoms back in our desert encounter.

The angelic audience gets a flash of insight that was yet to come for Christ's confused band of believers. They begin to see how God's justice is not sacrificed by his love but rather blends in a beautiful display of grace and holiness. They thought God was serious about sin in the Old Testament, with all its sacrifices, but that pales now in comparison to the sacrificial death of the Son of Man.

They reflect on the words of the Prophet Isaiah, "All of us like sheep have gone astray, Each of us has turned to his own way; But the LORD has caused the iniquity of us all To fall on Him" (Isa. 53:6). The sin issue is no trivial matter. The "iniquity" issue is not merely a violation of God's code of conduct, breaking the moral speed limit. The iniquity problem is captured in the statement of "each going their own way." Man's offense is an act of rebellion against his Creator, which has offended a holy God and caused his wrath. The crucifixion solution magnifies not only God's love but man's offense. Maybe man's sin is more like treason than breaking the speed limit?

At the crucifixion:

• The Son of Man becomes the promised Savior, the perfect sacrificial Lamb of God. A substitution was made: his death for our death, his righteousness for our unrighteousness – and all from grace. No spiritual calisthenics required, just a gift offered.

• The cross becomes the doorway into his new kingdom (John 14:6). The crucifixion is not the end but the beginning of the end.

In Israel's redemption from captivity in Egypt, they had to pass under the blood applied to their doorposts. It was their critical beginning to the Promised Land. It was so significant, to impress it on their collective consciousness, they were to celebrate it annually: The Passover. They were not to live in the doorway, but they were to remember its significance as they journeyed to freedom.

The Apostle Paul identifies a similar celebration on the resurrection side of the cross: The Lord's Supper.

For I received from the Lord that which I also delivered to you, that the Lord Jesus in the night in which He was betrayed took bread; and when He had given thanks, He broke it and said, "This is My body, which is for you; do this in remembrance of Me." In the same way He took the cup also after supper, saying, "This cup is the new covenant in My blood; do this, as often as you drink it, in remembrance of Me." For as often as you eat this bread and drink the cup, you proclaim the Lord's death until He comes (1 Cor. 11:23-26).

The angelic hosts never saw it coming. They had never seen such a display of undeserved love. At the cross, grace takes on flesh and blood, mercy is redefined, justice is maintained, and love becomes iridescent. The doorway to the kingdom is now open. The heavenly audience can hardly wait for the next Act to begin: "It's Friday, but Sunday's coming!"

For Reflection

1. What is the danger of the cross becoming the end rather than the doorway?

2. Contrast and compare the cross as substitutionary atonement and a doorway to the kingdom of light.

18

The Resurrection

For since by a man came death,
by a man also came the resurrection of the dead (1 Cor. 15:21)

As the curtain comes up on Act 4 (The Resurrection), a spotlight shines on a rock wall in a quiet garden. This scene is unique as it doesn't begin with Christ's presence but with his absence. We are unsure whether the heavenly audience knows what is about to happen or is as surprised as people in the story. Indeed, no one on stage has a clue.

On stage, a group of brave but cautious women approaches the grave where Jesus was buried a few days earlier. In their enthusiasm to finish treating the body of their crucified friend, they had not considered two tremendous obstacles: Roman guards and a massive stone. But when they arrive, they are delighted to see both removed. They have instant access.

However, when the women enter the tomb, their joy turns to surprise, confusion, amazement, and then fear. Jesus is gone! Will they or their friends be accused of robbing the grave? Suddenly a man dressed in white spoke to them, saying, "Do not be amazed; you are looking for Jesus the Nazarene, who has been crucified. He has risen; He is not here; behold, here is the place where they laid Him" (Mark 16:6). They were then instructed to go and "tell his disciples and Peter."

As Mark records the scene, he captures the range of emotions these women felt as they tried to digest what was happening.

They went out and fled from the tomb, for trembling and aston-

ishment had gripped them; and they said nothing to anyone, for they were afraid (Mark 16:8).

Returning to town, the women report the empty tomb and the angel's word of the risen Jesus to the apostles. Surprisingly the women are not met with joy and belief but with skepticism and adamant denial. The resurrection of Christ was not last on the disciples' list of possible outcomes; it wasn't even on the page. Later, when Mary Magdalene told the disciples that she had talked to the risen Christ, Mark says the disciples refused to believe it. However, their skepticism forced a few disciples to go to the grave and check it out for themselves. They return convinced: He has risen.

Over the next few months, not only does the news spread, but the risen Jesus appears to around 500 of his followers -- in person. When they heard, some believed right away; others needed additional proof. The Apostle Thomas was one of those hard to convince types, boldly claiming, "If I don't see him and touch him, I won't believe." For Thomas, sight preceded his faith, but Jesus tells him that from now on, faith will precede sight.

Our angelic audience must have been astonished to see the resurrected Son of God appear still in the human form of Jesus of Nazareth. He took up space, talked, ate, yet moved with ease in and out of the natural, physical dimension. Could it be that the risen Jesus is now the firstborn of a whole new kind of family, the first of many?

One thing is sure; the Son of Man conclusively demonstrated that he is the Son of God. Surely no one could doubt it now. Paul writes, "His Son, who was born of a descendant of David according to the flesh, who was declared the Son of God with power by the resurrection from the dead, according to the Spirit of holiness, (is) Jesus Christ our Lord" (Romans 1:1-4).

Excitement fills the angelic audience as the Son of God rises victorious over death. But they had seen similar events before throughout Biblical history, indeed rare but not unique. They remember those brought back to life in the Old Testament: the widow's son by Elijah (1 Kings 17:17+), the Shunammite's son by Elisha (2 Kings 4:18+). Now more recently, Jesus had raised a widow's son (Luke 7:11+), Jairus's daughter (Luke 8:52+), and his friend, Lazarus (John 11). Then at the time of the resurrection, a group of believers came out of their graves and entered Jerusalem, appearing and surprising many (Matt. 27:52).

These examples are impressive, but nothing compares to the resurrection of Jesus. All of those men and women who previously experienced a resurrection died again. Their resurrection was only temporary, a delay to the inevitable. But Jesus's resurrection was unique. His resurrection was with an incorruptible body. A body that was recognizable yet not subject to the natural laws of physics.

The disciples were excited when Jesus appeared to them after his resurrection, proving that he was indeed alive, but what was hard to comprehend was the "kind" of his appearance. He looked like the same Jesus. He spoke, and they touched him -- even the scars from the brutal crucifixion were tangible. But there was something supernatural about him now. He could walk in and out of their physical world with ease, not limited by walls or doors.

The Apostle Paul later described this new phenomenon as having an "incorruptible or imperishable" body (1 Cor. 15:50). The promise of being resurrected is difficult enough to comprehend, let alone being raised with a permanent body. Jesus was the first of a new kind of person. The resurrection promise for us is not only forgiveness and reconciliation, but the future reality of the corruptible body putting on the incorruptible.

Through the resurrection, he demonstrated his power, affirmed his deity, and established his kingdom. Victory is complete, death defeated, continuity guaranteed, and life is now eternal.

The resurrected Christ becomes a watershed moment in history, foolishness to most, but to a few, it is the hope of the future. This defining moment becomes a core part of the good news announced to a Gentile world. Speaking to the philosophers on Mar's Hill, Paul's mention of the resurrection drew a line in the sand. Some thought it ridiculous, others were curious, and a few believed. Nothing has changed in 2000 years!

For Reflection

1. What are other implications of the resurrection?

2. What is the significance of Paul's teaching that all will be raised: both the just and unjust (Acts 24:15)?

19

The Ascension

*While He was blessing them,
He parted from them
and was carried up into heaven* (Luke 24:51).

The fifth Act of His Story (The Ascension) begins in front of a closed curtain; the disciples gather around the risen Christ in earnest conversation. As they discuss what will happen next, Christ removes their ethnocentric lens by informing them that they will be his witnesses starting from Jerusalem and extending to the entire world. While the disciples reflect on the enormity of this mission, Jesus is "lifted up" and disappears from their sight (Acts 1:9).

As they stand there trying to comprehend what has just happened, two men in white clothing (typical description of angelic beings) confront them. They say, "You Galileans!—why do you just stand here looking up at an empty sky? This very Jesus who was taken up from among you to heaven will come as certainly—and mysteriously—as he left" (Acts 1:11 MSG). The disciples then walk down from the mountain, returning to Jerusalem with great joy (Luke 24:52).

As the disciples leave the front of the stage, the curtain opens, revealing the dimension called heaven. What appears center-stage is foreign to humanity but very familiar to our angelic audience. They celebrate as they observe heaven receiving back the Son of God. Only a few men have been given a glimpse into this dimension: Stephen, when he was stoned, Paul, when he had his vision and the Apostle John in the book of Revelation.

But what surprises our angelic audience is not that the Son of God has returned to heaven, but that he has returned while still identified with humanity. He remains the God/Man in his resurrected form. Christ has chosen to remain identified with humanity even to the point of retaining the scars of his crucifixion. Humanity has now entered heaven for the first time, demonstrating that the incarnation has no expiration date.

The ascension means that a human being rules the universe. [1]

The angels remember Jesus saying, "God so loved the world that he gave his only Son," and they now realize that the giving is more than just for a brief moment in history and more than the separation on the cross; he was given forever. From the incarnation into eternity, the Son of God wrapped himself in humanity. Jesus chose not to return to his pre-incarnation state of glory but to remain identified with those who are becoming his new covenant family.

The ascension tells us the resurrected life is permanent. Unlike Lazarus and Jairus' daughter, who overcame death only to die again, Christ's resurrection is made perpetual, eternal, and enduring. The sting of death is eradicated; hope takes its place.

Christ is both the sacrifice and the final High Priest. He takes his offering into the Holy of Holies and presents it to the Father. The ultimate sacrifice is completed--finished. In heaven, the ascended Christ becomes the representative and intercessor for his expanding family of faith. Now each child of God can come to the throne of grace with confidence at any time.

Therefore, since we have a great high priest who has passed through the heavens, Jesus the Son of God, ...Therefore let us draw near with confidence to the throne of grace (Heb. 4:14-16).

The ascended Christ is now our mediator, giving us direct access to the Father. Jesus told the disciples in the upper room that "Until now you have asked for nothing in My name; ask and you will receive, so that your joy may be made full" (John 16:24). "In my name" is more than a phrase tacked onto the end of a prayer; it is praying from the position of Christ's full authority. The idea of prayer is not new, but prayer claiming the authority of the ascended God/Man is new.

In the final moments of the Ascension Act, one more momentous event takes place. The Spirit of Christ is released to be the Son's representative on earth, living in the hearts of his new family. Releasing the Holy Spirit fulfills Jesus' promise made in the upper room, only a few weeks earlier. The Spirit brings power into the lives of men and women of faith, testifying, reminding, empowering, and guaranteeing their place with him forever. After the ascension, following Christ is no longer a matter of personal determination but abiding cooperation with the indwelling Spirit of Christ. His disciples are "in him," and he is "in them."

Luke ends his Gospel and begins the book of Acts with a description of the ascension, telling us that:

- At the cross, the disciples were scared, confused, and apprehensive.
- At the resurrection, they were surprised, amazed, and excited.
- At the ascension, however, they were filled with joy.

In this defining moment, God's reveals his manifold wisdom as humanity enters heaven, announcing:

- The incarnation has no expiration date,
- His sacrifice is accepted,
- Reconciliation is possible,
- The Holy Spirit is personal,
- Intercession is direct, and
- Christ becomes the elder brother.

Sadly the ascension has attracted little attention in today's Christianity. Most gospel presentations stop with the resurrection, as though the story ends there. Historically we have not always neglected the ascension. Until recently, the Apostle's Creed was a prominent part of church worship and liturgy. It was an early, historical statement of what Christians believed.

A modern version in part says:

> I believe in Jesus Christ, his only Son, our Lord.
> He was conceived by the power of the Holy Spirit
> and born of the Virgin Mary.
> He suffered under Pontius Pilate,
> was crucified, died, and was buried.
> He descended to the dead.
> On the third day he rose again.
> He ascended into heaven,
> and is seated at the right hand of the Father.
> He will come again to judge the living and the dead.

Notice that the ascension is as prominent as all the other defining moments in His Story.

The ascension was not insignificant to our heavenly audience. As they sit pondering the significance of all that has just happened, I can imagine them wondering, "Can anyone ever again doubt God's incredible love for humanity or question his delight in the expanding family born through faith?

[1] Tim Keller

For Reflection

1. Why do you think the disciples had joy at the ascension?

2. Why do most of our gospel presentations stop with the resurrection?

20

The Coronation

Therefore let all the house of Israel know for certain
that God has made Him both Lord and Christ—
this Jesus whom you crucified. (Acts 2:36)

The angels marvel as they witnessed the expanding revelation of the wisdom of God through the gospel narrative. They see the Son of God invade human history and witness multi-faceted aspects of God's nature revealed in new ways through his incarnation, demonstration, crucifixion, resurrection, and ascension. Their response is one of adoration, worship, and praise.

At the ascension, the Son of God returns to heaven as the eternal God/man, becoming the final High Priest forever linked to the humanity he created and loves. But wait, there is more. Drum roll, please! As the curtain opens for Act 6, The Coronation, the audience rises. The ascended Christ steps into the spotlight of heaven, taking his seat of authority at the right hand of the Father.

God, after He spoke long ago to the fathers in the prophets in many portions and in many ways, in these last days has spoken to us in His Son, whom He appointed heir of all things, through whom also He made the world. And He is the radiance of His glory and the exact representation of His nature, and upholds all things by the word of His power. When He had made purification of sins, He sat down at the right hand of the majesty on high (Heb. 1:1-3).

His coronation may not be a big deal to us, but it was in heaven. Old Testament prophecy is fulfilled as there is now a King forever on the throne of David. The Apostle John gives us a picture of Christ's coronation.

Then I looked, and I heard the voice of many angels around the throne and the living creatures and the elders; and the number of them was myriads of myriads, and thousands of thousands, saying with a loud voice, "Worthy is the Lamb that was slain to receive power and riches and wisdom and might and honor and glory and blessing (Rev. 5:11-12).

Earlier in the narrative, Christ's claim to be the King of a new kingdom brought several pseudo coronations. One was during the "Passion Week" leading up to Christ's crucifixion. In fulfillment of Old Testament prophecy, the King rides into Jerusalem among the cheers of a confused and desperate crowd.

Rejoice greatly, O daughter of Zion! Shout in triumph, O daughter of Jerusalem! Behold, your King is coming to you; He is just and endowed with salvation, Humble, and mounted on a donkey, Even on a colt, the foal of a donkey (Zech. 9:9).

For those who wanted an earthly king, the donkey was an embarrassment. They didn't think it was a very bold statement to Rome. Their more significant problem, however, was that Jesus wasn't stepping up to the challenge. Then they remembered another time when there was a popular movement to make him King. He wasn't interested then either (John 6:15).

A second pseudo-coronation happens when Pilate asks Jesus if he sees himself as a king. Answering in the affirmative, Jesus further explains that his kingdom, however, is not of this world: not the kind of kingdom Pilate had in mind. Trapped by his options, Pilate playing to the crowd, allows the Roman soldiers to stage a mocking coronation (John 19). With a twisted crown of thorns and a purple robe, they shout scornfully, "Hail, King of the Jews."

After the ascension, on the Day of Pentecost, Peter delivers the first gospel presentation to a large group of Jews from around the world. After working his way through the narrative of Christ, Peter lands on the coronation as his ultimate destination. It is like everything in the story has pointed to this anticipated event.

This Jesus God raised up again, to which we are all witnesses. Therefore having been exalted to the right hand of God ... For it was not David who ascended into heaven, but he himself says: 'THE LORD SAID TO MY LORD, SIT AT MY RIGHT HAND, UNTIL I MAKE YOUR ENEMIES A FOOTSTOOL FOR YOUR FEET' (Acts 2:32-35).

Peter then draws the obvious conclusion: "Therefore let all the house of Israel know for certain that God has made Him both Lord and Christ--this Jesus whom you crucified" (Act 2:36). Jesus, the Christ, no longer an itinerate teacher walking around on the fringes of society, is now the Lord/King over his kingdom and the cosmos.

Christ's coronation was central to Paul's message to the early church and part of his gospel.

These are in accordance with the working of the strength of His might which He brought about in Christ, when He raised Him from the dead and seated Him at His right hand in the heavenly places, far above all rule and authority and power and dominion, and every name that is named, not only in this age but also in the one to come. And He put all things in subjection under His feet, and gave Him as head over all things to the church (Eph. 1:19-23).

Jesus references his coronation when he introduces the "Great Commission." "All authority has been given to Me in heaven and on earth. Go therefore and make disciples" (Matt. 28:18-20). His authority gave those early disciples the boldness to defy the officials and proclaim the gospel.

As the Son of God returns to the heavens and takes control, the angelic audience rejoices. Never doubting his power or authority; they now see his leadership through a more transparent lens of grace, mercy, and love. While they are taking it all in, they are also perplexed -- baffled at the response of God's family of faith on earth and confused at the casual indifference to the King and his kingdom. They cannot understand why this new family of faith, having been born into God's family, and given citizenship in Christ's kingdom, live as though Jesus is just a teacher with some suggestions.

Christ now sits at the right hand of the Father. The Servant has become King, the Lamb is now the Lion, the kingdom firmly established, and hope is guaranteed. The church has a Head, and everything in heaven and earth is subject to him -- forever. Although his rule is currently invisible on planet earth, it is genuine in the heavens and the hearts of his disciples.

There is a day coming when his kingdom will become visible. He will return with power, majesty, and a final solution. Every eye will see him and acknowledge his authority; some will respond with praise while others with fear. But that will need to wait for our final Act: The Examination.

For Reflection

1. What can happen if the coronation is missing from our gospel presentation?

2. Why do our gospel presentations usually include only the crucifixion and resurrection?

21

The Examination

For we must all appear before the judgment seat of Christ,
so that each One may be recompensed for his deeds in the body,
according to what he has done, whether good or bad (2 Cor. 5:10).

The angelic audience, witnessing His Story's epic drama, now shifts its focus from what is happening to what will happen in the future. In this final Act, sometimes called the Revelation, Christ returns to earth in glory. He left quietly; he returns triumphantly!

As this Act plays out on the stage of history, the music will crescendo to a climax as the Son of Man (the previously invisible King) takes his place as King Victorious. Accompanied by the hosts of heaven, he will appear with great power, splendor, and glory for all to see. At his return, the living and the dead, the righteous and the unrighteous -- all will behold him (John 5:28-29); no one will be excluded. When he appears, there will be no doubt who he is.

He returns as the victorious King and the Bridegroom for his bride and as the righteous Judge. The angels know enough of the script to anticipate this event with joy and sorrow -- joy because they will announce his return and sorrow because they will execute his divine justice.

The angels know that their task is to separate those who have a "kingdom passport" from those who don't. Every person's passport will identify his/her spiritual birth date and citizenship. People will be citizens either of the domain of darkness or the kingdom of light. The offer to become a citizen of Christ's kingdom is no longer on the table. There is no second chance, and annihilation is not an option. The angels know they will escort one group into the eternal presence of God and the other into a destiny without him.

The anticipated display of the righteous wrath of God is sobering. Sobering because despite the clear evidence around them, people refuse to believe, choosing darkness instead of light and slavery instead of freedom. They are warned, yet they reject the message. They blow it off, rationalize it away, and try to make God into the caricature of Santa Clause. Maybe they think that justice delayed means it will never come, but in this Act the righteous Judge is here, and God's justice will be revealed.

In light of Scriptural teaching about this final Act, the angels are greatly perplexed. How can people claim that God's love will "win out," as though God's nature can be compartmentalized, enabling certain traits to trump others? Do they think that God's love has more power/authority than his justice?

Believers are perplexing as well. Why would people (especially those who read Scripture) be so cavalier about this final defining moment? Why do people live as though there is no continuity between their current life and the next? Where is the sense of accountability? Do they think grace has wiped out responsibility?

The scriptures are clear: each person will be responsible for the one life he/she has been given. There will be no excuses, alibies, or defenses. The assessment will be personal, thorough, accurate, and fair.

Do not be deceived, God is not mocked; for whatever a man sows, this he will also reap (Gal. (6:7).

Perhaps the concept of accountability was so essential to Paul because his life's ambition was to, first of all, please the One who had called him. To Paul, accountability was more than the gain or loss of rewards; it was the desire to delight the One he had come to know. To Paul, pleasing Jesus Christ (not to be confused with appeasing him) was the central motivation for living as his ambassador. For each of us as well, will not our greatest reward be to hear the words, "Well done, good and faithful servant" (Matt. 25:21).

In this final Act, all humanity will see his return in power and glory. Finally, the ascended Christ will be revealed as the sovereign King and righteous Judge. The epic drama of history will be comprehended, justice served, and stewardship rewarded. The Book will be opened, hypocrisy, and faithfulness will be celebrated. His family/his bride will be permanently transformed into a new expression of humanity, one that perfectly fits the new dimensions of the eternal home.

When the stage curtain closes this time, the post-production party begins. The star of the drama, the Son of God -- the Lord Jesus Christ, will hand over the kingdom and all the Oscars to the Father. The family of faith will witness this splendid celebration and express worship in the language and music of his/her own culture.

Although the curtain will come down on this epic drama, it is not the end. It is only the beginning. With sin abolished, Satan banished, and time irrelevant, the journey of knowing him will continue forever in a renewed and recreated universe.

Summary: His Story

Event	Place	Role
Act 1	Incarnation	Womb	Son of Man
Act 2	Demonstration	Israel	Servant

Act 3	Crucifixion	Cross	Savior
Act 4	Resurrection	Tomb	Victor
Act 5	Ascension	Heaven	High Priest
Act 6	Coronation	Throne room	King
Act 7	Examination	Courtroom	Judge

For Reflection

1. What is the difference between pleasing and appeasing?

2. What role does the final *Examination* play in your current life of discipleship?

22

Kingdoms in Conflict

For He rescued us from the domain of darkness,
and transferred us to the kingdom of His beloved Son (Col. 1:13).

Our culture has shifted seismically in the past few decades, leaving our audience at a different starting point for the gospel. Four cultural characteristics need consideration as we seek to articulate the gospel message (His Story) to our current world.

- **Biblically illiterate**

This generation knows very little of the Bible's primary story-line, including the people, stories, or events. They have heard of Jesus but know little of his essential claims and the narrative of his life.

- **Narcissistic**

Beyond consumerism, narcissism is selfishness on steroids. The general question asked is, "What's in it for me?"

- **Humanistic**

The essential elements of a biblical worldview have, for centuries, been the framework for understanding life, but they are now crumbling. We cannot assume our audience sees God as the uncaused Cause: the sovereign Creator and Sustainer of all that is (the cosmos). In our present culture, man is not the crown of God's creation or the focus of his love. Heaven and hell are just part of medieval fantasy.

- **Feeling based**

Facts and the logical pursuit to discover the truth are less relevant. "What I feel is my reality. No one can argue or debate it. "If I feel it, it's true."

Sean McDowell, associate professor of apologetics at Biola University, writes, "Authority has shifted from what is true to the feelings and beliefs of the individual. Feelings now trump truth."[+]

Past generations understood a biblical worldview regarding the relationship between God, man, sin, and Jesus. The role of evangelism was to clarify what it meant to believe the gospel or receive Christ. People already had the raw material with which to build on. They had pieces of the gospel but hadn't put them together. People did know, understood, and generally accepted the historical, biblical back story. We can no longer assume this is true.

Today we need to present a complete picture of who Jesus is and what he came to do. We need to set the gospel in its historical context if it is the powerful gospel that transfers and transforms lives (Romans 1:16, Col. 1:13). This gospel is more than a promise of sin management, a fire insurance policy, or a promise of "the good life." The gospel promises a radical transfer of kingdoms and the personal transformation of lives to fit into that new kingdom reality.

We must resist presenting an abridged gospel to this generation. We need to revisit how the gospel was presented in the book of Acts when the early Christians took their counter-cultural message to a skeptical and even hostile audience. It was an audience that lacked a biblical framework in which to understand the gospel. We must follow their example and focus on the complete revelation of the Son of God (His Story) as the good news. His Story embodies the truths that will set people free.

We also need to resist the temptation to "sell" the gospel or make it more attractive by appealing to the current culture's values, i.e., quick, easy, and fun. We need to present what is accurate and complete, including aspects that may be difficult to accept. Rather than minimizing or apologizing for the message, we need to recognize that the gospel will always be counter-cultural.

Several aspects of our typical gospel presentation needs expanding.

1. A more accurate picture of man's fallen condition.
2. An expanded explanation of the narrative of Christ.
3. An explanation regarding redemption that includes personal reconciliation with God, a kingdom transfer, and transformation.

The following illustration is an example of an expanded gospel presentation.

The gospel delivers us from more than the issue of sin. It delivers us from the kingdom of darkness that is now in opposition to the kingdom of light. Becoming a citizen of his kingdom means a new identity with a new passport.

[1] Sean McDowell, Ph.D., assistant professor of Christian apologetics, Biola University. Article in Christian Research Journal, Vol 40, Number 04.

For Reflection

1. Which of the seven defining moments of the narrative of Christ is irrelevant to the gospel? Why?

2. How does a kingdom perspective impact discipleship?

GOD

Creator and Sustainer of the cosmos

Sovereignty   Love   Grace

Humanity as the
crown of creation

Kingdom of Darkness

Default condition

- Spiritually dead
- Alienated from God
- Rebellious
- Morally bankrupt
- Under God's disapproval
- Captives in kingdom of darkness

Son of God

JESUS CHRIST THE LORD

The Gospel: His Story

- The Incarnation
- The Demonstration
- The Crucifixion
- The Resurrection
- The Ascension
- The Coronation
- The Examination

Kingdom of Light

Faith reality

- New life -- Spiritual dimension
- New relationship -- Connected to God
- New authority – Aligned with God
- New power – Moral freedom
- New record – Forgiveness
- New citizenship -- Kingdom of light

For He rescued us from the domain of darkness, and transferred us to the kingdom of His beloved Son (Col. 1:13).

Response: Repentance and faith (Mark 1:15)

23

The Cross and the Crown

But grow in the grace and knowledge
of our Lord and Savior Jesus Christ.
To Him be the glory,
both now and to the day of eternity. Amen. (2 Peter 3:18).

The cross and the crown of Jesus represent two significant aspects of his work. The cross historically represents his humiliation period, which I have referred to as his incarnation, demonstration, and crucifixion. The crown represents his exaltation period, which I have identified as his resurrection, ascension, coronation, and examination.

Commonly, the cross summarizes his humiliation and role as Savior while the crown summarizes his exaltation: his kingdom and his role as King.

Historically, there has been a fragile tension between these two significant Christian faith elements: the cross and the crown. Because we tend to polarize what we cannot harmonize, we oscillate between these two truths rather than holding them in dynamic tension. The result has been called a *pendulum swinging reductionism.*[1]

Church history during the 20th century gives us several examples of this swinging reductionism. Early in the 1900s, social conditions, especially in the larger cities, were deplorable. Many mainline churches responded to this need with a "social gospel" of building the kingdom through social reform. Initially, it merely elevated the crown over the cross, but eventually, the theme of redemption was lost altogether.

As a reaction, "conservative" denominations bore down on the salvation message, ignoring or minimalizing the crown and the kingdom. In the past few decades, this tension has emerged again in what has been called the "missional movement." It focuses on the physical needs of our culture but often at the expense of the gospel.

Another form of this tension surfaced in the latter half of the 20th century with the debate over "Lordship Salvation." It pitted the view that a belief in Jesus as Savior was all that was necessary. The opposing view stressed the need to believe in him as Savior and to be committed to him as Lord.

An additional contributor to this tension is the influence of symbols. Throughout Christian and secular history, the cross has survived as the primary symbol of the Christian faith. It was not always this way. The cross was rarely used as a symbol during the first three hundred years of Christianity. Before Constantine, the early church used various symbols for faith.

The second-century Christian teacher Clement of Alexandria identified a dove, a fish, a ship, a lyre, and an anchor as suitable images to be engraved on Christians' signet-rings (or seals). [2]

Among the symbols employed by the early Christians, that of the fish seems to have ranked first in importance. Ichthus (ΙΧΘΥΣ, Greek for fish) is an acronym, a word formed from the first letters of several words. It translates to "Jesus Christ God's Son Savior," in ancient Greek. [3]

The symbol of the cross and crown together never quite caught on, which is unfortunate, in my opinion.

One reason could be that to draw a cross is much simpler than drawing a crown. It is relatively easy to make the "sign of the cross," but to make the "sign of the crown" would take a lot more coordination. Just try it sometime! So maybe out of convenience, we disconnected the theme of the kingdom of God from the atonement.

The cross and the crown tension is also illustrated as one Christian organization focuses on social needs, another on evangelism, while another on discipleship. In the 1950s, during the early years of the Billy Graham Crusades, Graham recognized the need for discipleship. Because of his calling to evangelism, he asked Dawson Trotman, founder of The Navigators, for help. He asked the Navigators to develop a way to "follow up" the new converts streaming forward at the Crusades. Graham understood these people needed not only the cross but also the crown: evangelism and discipleship.

To help maintain a healthy dynamic between the cross and the crown, we need to remember that Christ's atonement has both an individual and kingdom component. Through the cross, God dealt with man's rebellion to God's authority (sin), and God's wrath is averted. But the atonement also sets us free from the domain of the kingdom of darkness and transfers us into the kingdom of light: the kingdom of God's Son. Therefore, the cross results in both substitutionary atonement and also kingdom transfer. As we learn how to live in his kingdom (discipleship), we find new significance, identity, and responsibility.

I imagine the symbol of the cross originally carried with it the entire story of Jesus Christ, the Lord. But over time and changing cultures, it has lost the context of the kingdom. I am not crusading for a new, revised Christian symbol but rather a renewed union of the cross and the crown. When the cross and the crown are united in our minds as the gospel's central theme, then discipleship on the resurrection side of the cross will no longer be an elective but an essential and natural response.

[1] The practice of simplifying a complex idea, issue, condition, or the like, especially to the point of minimizing, obscuring, or distorting it. For more background, read *The Crucified King*, Jeremy Treat, Zondervan, pg. 26.

[2] *Christianity Today,* February 2009, "When did the cross supplant the ichthus (fish) as a symbol of the Christian faith?" Everett Ferguson.

[3] *New World Encyclopedia* "Christian Symbolism."

For Reflection

1. Which symbol of Christianity has most affected you?

2. How could we better reconnect the cross and the crown?

24

Grace and Conditions

And we know that God causes all things to work together
for good to those who love God,
to those who are called according to His purpose (Rom. 8:28).

The word grace is used over 170 times in the Greek translation of the New Testament with various meanings. Vines NT dictionary defines grace (charis) as that which bestows or occasions pleasure, delight, or causes favorable regard. In the Old Testament, the concept is expressed by the word "lovingkindness." It can refer to a person's external appearance, like "she carried herself with grace." But in our religious jargon, grace has come to mean the unmerited favor of God, expressed to us out of his loving nature.

We often add the word unconditional when talking about God's grace, saying, "God's grace is unmerited and unconditional." But is this statement accurate? When we read the promises in Scripture, most often they contain conditions, an "if-then" connection. If we take the conditions seriously, it can create tension with our concept of grace. How can a promise be gracious and yet conditional?

One solution is to ignore the conditions as irrelevant, more like religious hyperbole. Since we tend to polarize what we cannot harmonize, we often claim the promises but disregard the uncomfortable conditions. Consider a familiar promise from Scripture:

Be anxious for nothing, but in everything by prayer and supplication with thanksgiving let your requests be made known to God. And the peace of God, which surpasses all compre-hension, will guard your hearts and your minds in Christ Jesus (Phil. 4:6-7).

The promise is for the peace of God to guard our hearts and minds. It is unquestionably a gracious offer by God for our benefit, trading anxiety for peace? But the unmerited offer is prefaced by specific conditions: prayer, supplication, and thanksgiving!

So how do we handle the tension? The solution is not to ignore the conditions or minimize grace, but rather decouple the idea of conditions from the concept of merit. It is an unnecessary and detrimental alliance.

Some friends of ours recently called to offer us tickets to the Kansas City Symphony at the Kaufman Center. They said they were a gift if we wanted them. When we replied in the affirma-tive, they said we could pick them up at the "will call" window before the performance.

Arriving a little early to the concert, I went to the "will call" window and asked for the tickets reserved in my name. Once in hand, we eagerly (and gratefully) gave them to the usher and took our seats in the auditorium.

Nowhere along that process did I connect standing in line, ask-ing for the tickets, and presenting them to the usher as some form of merit. However, had I failed to do any of those things, we would not have benefited from the gracious gift. The tickets offered without merit required an action on my part for the gift to be experienced. The action was relatively trivial compared to the gift itself. The gift was free, but experiencing the gift was not automatic; it required a response.

Similarly, the gracious gift of reconciliation with God offered without merit (other than Christ's) is not unconditional. The familiar John 3:16 promise of "not perishing and have eternal life" is prefaced by the condition: Belief. Although we need to comply with the condition, we should not think that we are somehow meriting the gift by fulfilling it.

We also should not expect the gracious gifts of God without respecting the conditions connected to them. The conditions are never arbitrary but wisely given as a further expression of his character.

When our youngest son was about six years old, he came to me one day and asked if he could have his own "boys" bike. I asked him what was wrong with his sister's bike. He said, "Well, it's pink and has Smurfs all over it."

"What kind would you like?" I asked.

He replied immediately, "I want a black one with knobby tires!"

So I made him a promise: If he learned to ride his sister's bike without the training wheels, I would get him his own "boys" bike -- black with knobby tires.

The promise's condition was not to merit the bike as though he was earning money to buy it. The condition was given to encourage the development of a helpful life-skill (bike riding) that would benefit him beyond his current desire for a shiny new bike.

A few months later, he came to me to claim what I promised. After he rode the pink Smurf bike down the driveway without training wheels, we went to the store and picked out a cool, black bike with knobby tires.

In a much more significant way, God graciously offers us promises to live by that contain conditions. We must neither ignore them nor think of them as a form of merit. Instead, we should consider them part of God's plan to help us obediently walk with him by faith.

For Reflection

1. Which of God's promises are you claiming? What are their conditions?

2. What are the conditions to the promise in Rom. 8:28?

25

God's Iridescent Love

We have come to know and have believed the love
which God has for us. God is love,
and the one who abides in love abides in God,
and God abides in him (1 John 4:16).

Jesus loves me, this I know, for the Bible tells me so was the al-
leged response twentieth-century theologian Karl Barth gave
when asked to summarize his life's work in theology. The as-
tounding simplicity, magnitude, and beauty of the love of God
have amazed theologians, poets, and ordinary people down
through history.

However, while it is simple to say, God's love is not a simple
concept to understand or grasp.

The Apostle Paul did not believe the love of God was shallow or
straightforward. His prayer for the church was, "that you, being
rooted and grounded in love, may be able to comprehend with
all the saints what is the breadth and length and height and
depth, and to know the love of Christ which surpasses knowledge, that you may be filled up to all the fullness of God" (Eph.
3:17-19).

Paul believed that God's love is the foundation for faith and a
vast reality to be explored, but we need help. God's love is vast
and unknowable in its complexity, yet understandable in ever-
increasing degrees through the power of the Holy Spirit. Paul's
prayer for the Spirit to enhance our ability to grasp this remarkable aspect of God's nature indicates not only its importance
but its complexity. However, there are three major hindrances

to understanding his love.

First, I am concerned that in our current culture of sound bites and over-generalizations, we have trivialized and distorted this critically important quality of God so that it is no longer a wonder to pursue. Throughout our discipleship journey, Paul challenges us to think in terms of its vast magnitude and its incredible complexity. Comprehending God's love should be a central theme as we grow both in our love for God and our love for others.

D.A. Carson observes, *The doctrine of the love of God is sometimes portrayed within Christian circles as much easier and more obvious than it really is, and this is achieved by overlooking some of the distinctions the Bible itself introduces when it depicts the love of God.*[1]

Second, we are hindered in our journey to understand the depth of God's love by an inadequate vocabulary. Our single English word "love" covers a vast span of meanings. We "love" pizza, our dog, our children, our spouse, and even God, using one word in English for many expressions of love.

The Old Testament Hebrew language has two main words for love. The word *ahab* is equivalent to the English "to love" in the sense of having a strong emotional attachment and desire to possess an object or be in its presence. It is found in all periods of Hebrew writing and approximately 250 times in the Bible. The other word *checed* is often translated as loving-kindness and is a covenant term of relationship between God and Israel. It is a clear demonstration of grace over merit.[2]

With the revelation of God's redemptive love in Christ, the New Testament writers needed a new word that didn't have the emotional, romantic, or merit elements. Avoiding the Greek words *eros* (a physical love) and *pheleo* (an affectionate love), they chose a familiar (yet somewhat obscure) Greek word for love: *agape.*

The Greek dictionary (Thayer) defines AGAPE (agapao): to welcome, to entertain, to be fond of, to love dearly, to be well pleased with something.

To this general definition, New Testament writers added a more focused meaning. It referred to an "unconditional, self-sacrificing, giving love to all – both friend and enemy." [3] Adding to the complexity of understanding love in Scripture, *agape* is not always used in this more focused way. For example, Jesus said that he loved (*agapao*) the Father (John 14:31), using it in the sense of the general meaning rather than the focused one.

To avoid a monolithic view of God's love, theologians down through history have expressed the complexity of God's love by using various adjectives to describe it, including intra-Trinitarian, complacent[4], benevolent, compassionate, merciful, and affectionate.

Intra-Trinitarian love refers to the love that exists within the Trinity. John referred to this love when he said, "God is love" (1 John 4:8). God not only loves, but he is love. Love resides within the essence of who God is. John is not saying that God equals love, but rather that love is a trait of divinity (along with his other traits such as holiness and justice). Neither is John making love the "trump card" in the deck of God's attributes. Love is part of God's essence, permeating all his other characteristics, and is the source of love as we know it.

Therefore, it should not surprise us to see love expressed within the Trinity. Jesus described the Father's love for the Son as both agape (John 3:35) and pheleo (John 5:20). He describes his love for the Father in John 14:31. "I will do what the Father requires of Me, so that the world will know that I love (agape) the Father."

Jesus now invites us into this intimate intra-Trinitarian love. In his prayer in John 17, Jesus prays that his disciples would come to experience this same kind of love.

I have made your name known to them, and will make it known, so that the love with which You love Me may be in them, and I in them (John 17:26).

The characteristics of light in the physical world can illustrate the unity and complexity of God's love. White light appears to be colorless, for example, ordinary daylight. It is "white" when it contains all the wavelengths of the visible spectrum at equal intensity. White light illustrates the "simplicity" of light. But light isn't simple. It is, in reality, complex consisting of all the colors of the rainbow.

Intra-Trinitarian love is like "white light" that contains various frequencies or expressions. As white light produces a rainbow of colors as it passes through a prism, God's love reveals its color complexity as it touches the prism of broken humanity. We are like a diamond or prism that God shapes to reflect the brilliance of his love in all its vibrant colors.

As we observe, understand, and experience the various colors of God's love, it should fill us with wonder and gratitude, amazed at both its magnitude and complexity.

A third hindrance to our understanding of God's love is our refusal to respond to it. Without some expression, we will not know that love exists. Similarly, we will not experience an expression of love without a response. Jesus explains that within the Trinity, both love's expression and response are evident.

For the Father loves the Son, and shows him all things that he himself is doing (John 5:20).

But so that the world may know that I love the Father, I do exactly as the Father commanded Me (John 14:31).

In John 3:16, Jesus explains that God expresses his love by giving his only begotten Son, but to experience that love, we must respond by "believing in him."

In the following reflections, I want to explore the beautiful, iridescent expressions of the love of God through the primary colors of what I will call his:

- Creative, sustaining love,

- Personal redemptive love,

- Family covenant love, and

- Intimate friendship love.

---

[1] The Difficult Doctrine of the Love of God DA Carson, pg.15
[2] International Standard Bible Encyclopedia (ISBE)
[3] New World Encyclopedia, electronic version
[4] Complacent in classical use does not mean passivity, but a love towards that which pleases.

For Reflection

1. Can you relate to a situation where love was expressed, but there was no response?

2. How do you respond to the statement, "Love is conditional?"

26

God's Refracted Love

I am in them and You are in Me.
May they experience such perfect unity that
the world will know that You sent Me
and that You love them as much as You love Me (John 17:23).

The iridescent colors of God's love are displayed as they pass through the prism of our broken humanity. Our God desires that we know and experience the greatness of his love both in its magnitude and complexity. As the white light of God's love shines in, and through us, it is both refracted (broken into its various colors) and reflected.

Down through history, theologians have used various terms to describe the complexity of God's love: benevolent, beneficent, and complacent. Keep in mind that this complexity does not sacrifice the unity of his love any more than the four New Testament Gospel accounts destroy the gospel's unity. I want to highlight four colors (expressions) of God's love, referring to them as his:

- Creative sustaining love,
- Personal redemptive love,
- Family covenant love, and
- Intimate relational love.

All of God's creation displays his **creative, sustaining love** (sometimes referred to as his providential love). Creation itself is an expression of who God is and thereby reveals his nature to everyone, everywhere, all the time. In the book "Privileged Planet," the authors identify the remarkable uniqueness of our celestial planet and note its critical position in our galaxy, making it possible for us to observe the vast cosmos around us. So why should our planet be in this unique place? Could it be that God wants us to observe the universe because it reflects his creative, sustaining love?

All of humanity, even those who reject him, are recipients of God's creative, sustaining love. Jesus said, "He causes his sun to rise on the evil and the good, and sends rain on the righteous and the unrighteous" (Matt. 5:45). God expresses his creative love to all, but not everyone acknowledges it.

For since the creation of the world God's invisible qualities...have been clearly seen being understood from what has been made, ... For even though they knew God, they did not honor Him as God or give thanks, but they became futile in their speculations, ... and exchanged the glory of the incorruptible God for an image in the form of corruptible man (Romans 1:20-23).

The cosmos is an expression of God's creative, sustaining love and provides the platform for understanding his redemptive love. Because of the importance of this connection, we should not be surprised at Satan's strategy to separate God from creation in most people's minds. "Macroevolution is an arrow in the heart of the gospel." [1]

His **personal redemptive love** is expressed through the gospel, specifically by Christ's death on the cross. Calvary made atonement possible for all humanity, given without merit but not, however, without conditions. In John 3:16, God expresses his redemptive love and our necessary response.

The Hebrew Passover illustrates redemptive love. God graciously redeemed a chosen people from slavery in Egypt. God offered this expression of his love without merit but not without conditions. The Hebrews would experience this redemptive love only if they placed the blood of a lamb over the door of their home and followed Moses out of Egypt.

Redemptive love is the expression of love that leads us to the third color: his **family covenant love.**

God expresses this love through our new identity and position in Christ (2 Corinthians 5:17). Introduced in passages like John 1:12 and 1 John 3:1-3, this covenant family love is revealed in God's gifts of adoption, citizenship, and the indwelling of the Holy Spirit. The result is we have a new position and identity expressed in all the rights and privileges found in Christ (Eph. 1:3-11), including our future inheritance as heirs with Christ.

A biblical example of covenant family love is God's relationship with the people of Israel. Calling them his family, people, and vineyard, the Old Testament tells this family's story and their arduous journey to discover God's covenant love. Within this love, Israel was to learn to obey and follow God. Their struggle to respond to God's covenant love is an instructive but sad story, serving as a warning for us who now live under the new covenant of God's family love.

The fourth expression of God's iridescent love is his **intimate relational love**. This expression exposes us to the very heart of God and is the most intimate of all the expressions. It is a relational love modeled within the Trinity.

We see this expression in the life of Jesus with his 12 disciples. Once they responded to his call to follow, they experienced an increasing intimacy with him. The crowds experienced his miracles, but the disciples experienced his relational, intimate love. Christ allowed Peter, James, and John, the privilege of even deeper intimacy as they witnessed both the glory of his transfiguration and the agony of his prayer in the Garden.

The original disciples also experienced this relational love in the upper room just before the trial and crucifixion. In those final hours, they heard and saw first-hand the passion of Christ to fulfill the Father's plan and purpose. They were allowed to listen in on the intimate conversation between Jesus and the Father, as recorded in John 17.

The relational, intimate love shown to the disciples didn't just happen; it was the result of their growing allegiance to and alignment with his person and mission.

I have loved you even as the Father has loved Me. Remain in My love. When you obey My commandments, you remain in My love, just as I obey My Father's commandments and remain in His love. I have told you these things so that you will be filled with My joy. Yes, your joy will overflow.... You are My friends if you do what I command. I no longer call you slaves, because a master doesn't confide in His slaves. Now you are My friends, since I have told you everything the Father told Me (John 15:9-15).

[1] Jim Sorensen

For Reflection

1. How are these expressions of God's love related to each other?

2. How do you see these expressions of God's love demonstrated in God's relationship with Old Testament Israel?

27

God's Love Language

If you keep My commandments, you will abide in My love;
just as I have kept My Father's commandments and abide in His love
(John 15:10).

When asked about the greatest commandment, Jesus answered, "Love the Lord your God with all your heart, mind, and strength." However, what does loving God look like? Is it merely having positive thoughts or feelings about God? Can we choose our preferred way to love God?

Previously, I suggested that it takes both expression and response for love to be known and experienced. Using the four expressions of God's love discussed previously, I want to explore the love response that God expects. Borrowing from the 1992 book by Gary Chapman, we need to respond according to his "love language."

Each expression of God's love is an outgrowth of his grace and is, therefore, given without human merit. However, we do not experience them automatically. While God's love is always unmerited, it is not always unconditional. God has established that each expression of his love requires a specific response. Our response in no way diminishes his grace. Each response takes us deeper into the heart of God, suggesting that we are as close to God as we choose to be.

To begin, the broadest expression of God's love is his creative, sustaining love. It is given without merit or condition and is evidenced by all that he has created. Even those who reject God are recipients of this love. In Romans 1, the Apostle Paul identifies the expected response to this expression of love should be reverence and gratitude. However, that is often not the case, as Paul explains.

For even though they knew God, they did not honor Him as God or give thanks, but they became futile in their speculations, and their foolish heart was darkened (Rom. 1:21).

God's next expression of love is his redemptive love, and it takes us deeper into the heart of God. This love expression releases people from captivity in the domain of darkness and brings them into the kingdom of light (Col. 1:13-14). Jesus refers to this love in the familiar John 3:16: "For God so loved the world." But to experience redemptive love, we must respond with repentance and belief in him (Mark 1:15; John 3:16). If we don't respond with those conditions, the love remains expressed, but we will not experience it.

God's family covenant love is an expression that takes us even deeper into our love relationship with God as we become his children (John 1:12; 1 John 3:1-3). God also expresses his family love through gifts such as justification, adoption, citizenship, and the indwelling of the Holy Spirit. The expected response to his family love is a life of alignment with God's will.

He who has My commandments and keeps them is the one who loves Me; and he who loves Me will be loved by My Father, and I will love him and will disclose Myself to him (John 14:21).

Obedience is not a condition to experience either God's creative or redemptive love, but it is a condition to experience his family love. Failure to distinguish the difference will result in requiring obedience for redemption (salvation by works) while ignoring obedience within the family.

The intimate relational love of God adds still another, more personal, and dynamic level of relationship. This expression of love is the continued revelation of himself as we walk in him (Col 2:6). Jesus talks about this expression of love with his disciples in the upper room discourse:

If you keep My commandments, you will abide in My love; just as I have kept My Father's commandments and abide in His love... You are My friends if you do what I command you. No longer do I call you slaves, for the slave does not know what his master is doing; but I have called you friends, for all things that I have heard from My Father I have made known to you (John 15:10-15).

This "friendship" love that was now part of the disciples' experience wasn't automatic. It came as a result of their continued alignment with Jesus and his kingdom, resulting in greater exposure to the heart and mind of God in Christ. I think this profoundly personal and relational love expression is what Jesus was asking for in John 17:

I have made Your name known to them, and will make it known, so that the love with which You loved Me may be in them, and I in them (John 17:26).

The offer of this expression of his love is humbling, even overwhelming to me, yet it is what God desires us to discover. It is what our souls look for but in all the wrong places.

The natural response to this intimate love of God is to enjoy his person and presence. It was what Mary was commended for in Luke 10: "Mary, who sat before the Master, hanging on every word he said ..." (MSG). It is a response of affection that desires God even without His blessings. Habakkuk expressed it this way:

Though the fig tree should not blossom And there be no fruit on the vines, Though the yield of the olive should fail And the fields produce no food, Though the flock should be cut off from the fold

And there be no cattle in the stalls, yet I will exult in the LORD, I will rejoice in the God of my salvation (Hab. 3:17-18).

Experiencing the increasing depth of God's iridescent love reminds me of the Russian Matryoshka dolls; each time we experience one expression of his love, we are exposed to an even deeper one. Our reward for responding is not prosperity but a deeper relationship. This wonderfully complex love of God invites us into a timeless relational journey Jesus called eternal life (John 17:3).

On the resurrection side of the cross, God calls us to experience the white light of his love in all of its various colors.

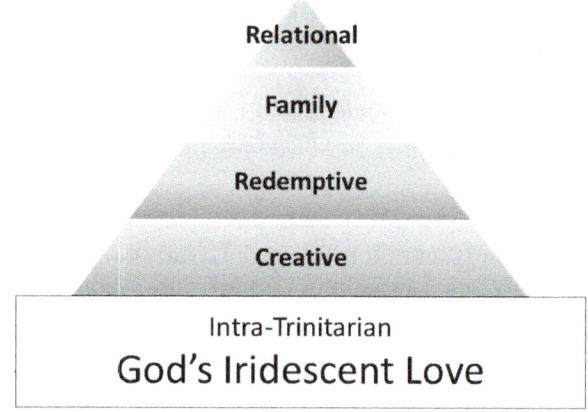

For Reflection

1. Each love expression has a unique response. What happens when we get them mixed up?

2. How is spiritual maturity related to these love expressions?

28

God's Reflected Love

Beloved, let us love one another, for love is from God;
and everyone who loves is born of God and knows God (1Jn. 4:7).

The power and manner in which we love others are rooted in our personal experience of God's love. His love enables us to understand what real love means and empowers us to put it into practice. We are not the source of love but the reflectors of God's iridescent love.

Jesus said that one mark of being his disciple is loving others. He even called it a new commandment.

So now I am giving you a new commandment: Love each other.
Just as I have loved you, you should love each other (John 13:34;
15:12).

What made this commandment new was not the substance (love people) but the model (as I have loved you). In the Old Testament, the model was self-love: loving others as we love ourselves. Since we are conspicuously self-centered, self-absorbed, and narcissistic, our self-love applied to others is a high standard. However, Jesus modeled a much higher standard: love in the way he loves. Only by the gospel's transforming power are we set free to go beyond self-love to Christ-like love.

We have discussed four ways God expresses his iridescent love and how we should respond to each one. Now let's look at how to love others in those same ways. Principle: God commands us to love others but not everyone in the same way.

1. Love others with the sustaining love of God.

This form of love is expressed to everyone without merit and conditions. It is the kind of love Jesus refers to in the "Sermon on the Mount."

You have heard the law that says, 'Love your neighbor' and hate your enemy. But I say, love your enemies! [Bless those who curse you. Do good to those who hate you.] Pray for those who persecute you! In that way, you will be acting as true children of your Father in heaven. For He gives His sunlight to both the evil and the good, and He sends rain on the just and the unjust alike (Matt. 5:43-45 NLT).

Benevolent acts of kindness demonstrate this form of love without regard to merit or visible reward. This expression of love shines brightest when the recipient is notably unworthy. It radiates grace and mercy.

2. Love others with redemptive love.

The ultimate example of redemptive love is God's love expressed by the sacrificial death of Christ on the cross. So how do we express his redemptive love to others? Consider the following three ways as a starting point.

• Love others as ambassadors, sharing the gospel of reconciliation by boldly modeling and declaring the narrative of God's redemptive love in Christ.

• As forgivers forgiving those who seek forgiveness. Peter asked the critical question, "How many times should we forgive?" Jesus response gives several guidelines (Luke 17:3-4):

    1. If your brother sins rebuke him.
    2. If he repents, forgive him.
    3. If he sins seven times in the day and turns to you

(meaning repents), forgive him seven times.

Another way to offer forgiveness is not to take offense in the first place. Too often, our "injustice" detector is way too sensitive. In the classic description of love, Paul tells us intentionally choose not to be offended.

Love is patient, love is kind and is not jealous; love does not brag and is not arrogant, does not act unbecomingly; it does not seek its own, is not provoked, does not take into account a wrong suffered (emphasis mine) (1 Cor. 13:4-5).

We can offer redemptive love to many people if we can learn to "let it go," absorbing the wrong by not taking offense.

- *Love others as peacemakers, bringing harmony to our fractured world* (Matt 5:9).

People who love others this way seek opportunities to bring people together. They take a personal risk to reduce friction, bring perspective, and foster dialogue. Peacemakers lower the temperature in the room and radiate hope. They don't suppress friction or ignore it, but their attitude and words of encouragement can provide an atmosphere that calms the storm.

3. Love others with a family love.

Behold, what manner of love the Father has bestowed upon us, that we should be called the sons of God (1 John 3:1).

John is referring to the family love of the Father. God doesn't extend this kind of love to humanity in general, but to his family. It was the particular kind of love he offered Israel as his chosen people. God did not love all nations in the same way. In the New Testament, Jesus's new command focused on "one another." John calls it loving the family of faith (I John 4:11). An example would be Paul's collection of money for saints in

Jerusalem during a famine. It was specifically for the saints in Jerusalem who were suffering. Although believers were not the only ones affected by this famine, the collection from the churches in Asia Minor was specifically designated to support the family of faith.

4. Love others with a relational love.

After three-plus years with the disciples, Jesus called them his friends. By this time, his relationship with them was closer than what he had with the crowds -- even the 70. Peter, James, and John shared an even closer relationship than did the other disciples, and it appears that John may have been the closest of all.

The relationship between Jonathan and David in the Old Testament comes close to illustrating this kind of authentic friendship love. Paul and Timothy also seem to share this kind of relationship (Phil. 2:19-20). A relational love is developed over time when accompanied by trust, respect, and shared experiences. This expression of love will not develop without both intentionality and vulnerability.

John reminds us that loving others is a command, not an option. "This is My commandment: Love each other in the same way (emphasis mine) I have loved you" (John 15:12 NLT). Jesus refracts his iridescent, divine love through our lives so that we can reflect that same kind of love to others.

For Reflection

1.   How do you respond to the idea that we are to love everybody but not everybody in the same way?

2.   What limits our ability to love with a personal love?

29

Knowing is more than Knowledge

Yes, everything else is worthless
when compared with the infinite value
of knowing Christ Jesus my Lord (Phil. 3:8).

For several months I was having a spiritual conversation with a physician friend of mine. One day in frustration, he said, "I don't get it. You (and those like you) talk about a personal relationship with Christ. That doesn't make sense to me. How can you have a "personal relationship" with an invisible God?"

His response surprised me and made me think about how casually I use that term without thinking about it or explaining it. It does sound strange. No other religion claims that its followers can relate to God in a personal way.

Wanting to explain the concept, I realized that the phrase "personal relationship" is not used in Scripture, but neither is the word "Trinity." However, the idea of relating to God on an individual and personal level is everywhere. It would be presumptuous, even preposterous, was it not taught in Scripture as a reality.

Since this idea is central to discipleship, let's stop and look at its use in Scripture. "Knowing" is a term in the New Testament that implies more than information; it carries the idea of a personal relationship. "Vines Expository Dictionary of New Testament Words" explains it like this:

GIN0SKO (GK) signifies "to be taking in knowledge, to come to know, recognize, understand," or "to understand completely." In the NT ginosko frequently indicates a relation between the person "knowing" and the object known; in this respect, what is "known" is of value or importance to the one who knows, and hence the establishment of the relationship.

Eternal life, which we usually think of as a condo in heaven, Jesus refers to as knowing him. "This is eternal life, that they may know You, the only true God, and Jesus Christ whom You have sent" (John 17:3). The implication is that eternal life is more a relationship term than a place; it begins at the moment of our new birth and continues throughout eternity.

Jesus tells an uncomfortable story in the Sermon on the Mount. "Not everyone who calls out to Me, 'Lord! Lord!' will enter the Kingdom of Heaven. Only those who do the will of My Father in heaven will enter. On judgment day many will say to Me, 'Lord! Lord! We prophesied in Your name and cast out demons in Your name and performed many miracles in Your name.' But I will reply, 'I never **knew** (emphasis mine) you. Get away from Me, you who break God's laws.' "(Matt. 7:21-23 NLT). The key to the kingdom is not what we say or what we do, but whom we know.

So how do we know Christ? What does knowing mean when dealing with God, who is both transcendent and invisible? The Bible even talks about the possibility of knowing him as we would a personal friend. Moses is one of the Old Testament persons referred to as a friend of God. "Inside the Tent of Meeting, the LORD would speak to Moses face to face, as one speaks to a friend" (Exod. 33:11). How is that possible? (See also Isa. 41:8; James 2:23)

King David, a giant example of a person who cultivated a relationship with God, is singled out by God for their close relationship. God's epitaph for David, found in Acts 13:22, says, "After He had removed him (King Saul), He raised up David to be their king, concerning whom He also testified and said, 'I

HAVE FOUND DAVID the son of Jesse, A MAN AFTER MY HEART, who will do all My will.'"

We can better understand the meaning of this relational knowing by comparing it with other things we know. For example, we learn about a rock by studying its composition. With a microscope, chemicals, and some diligence, we can learn many facts about a rock. Geologists can give us the history of the rock, its formation, composition, and uses. Although well informed, we would still not claim to have a relationship with the rock.

Reading about a person, past or present, is another form of knowing. Biographers study and write about the life of a person so we can know about him or her. Based on the biographer's historical record's reliability, we can get a reasonably accurate picture of a person's life and character, but the knowledge is second or third hand.

The biblical idea of knowing Christ (God) is more than knowing his composition (character and attributes) or the storyline (the biblical narrative). It is a personal relationship in the same way we would know any living person except, of course, that God is invisible.

There is a danger that we settle for knowing Christ as we would know any other historical figure. We study about him, even marvel at his attributes, but fail to know him experientially. We can explore the narrative of what he did, become familiar with what he said, even learn what others said about him, and still not know him.

A relational knowing requires critical elements. I want to suggest four, which we will discuss in the next Reflection.

They are:

- Mutual respect

- Consistent dialogue

- Shared experiences

- Authentic transparency

For Reflection

1. How have the four critical elements above developed or hindered a relationship you have with another person?

2. Which of the four is the hardest for you and why?

30

Free but not Automatic

But only one thing is necessary,
for Mary has chosen the good part,
which shall not be taken away from her (Luke 10:42).

The privilege of a relational connection with Christ on the resurrection side of the cross is possible only by grace through faith in the person and work of Christ. Paul refers to this new connection as Christ "in us" and we "in him." This new reality offers us the opportunity to develop a deeply personal relationship with our Lord, which Paul called: to know him. This possibility is an incredible gift. However, we do not experience this kind of relationship without intentionality. It is neither automatic nor a one-time event. Instead, it requires consistent daily effort and practice.

As mentioned in Reflection #4, the process of knowing Christ is similar to developing our relationship with any living person. Let's consider four critical elements that will help us relate experientially.

Mutual respect

The Cambridge Dictionary defines respect as "admiration felt or shown for someone or something that you believe has good ideas or qualities." We may respect someone we do not know, but we will rarely have a personal relationship with someone we do not respect and trust. A stable and deep connection involves mutual respect. It must go both ways.

Understanding and admiration of his true nature are critical to our relationship with Christ. This understanding is more than knowledge of his divine nature, such as his omniscient, omnipresent, and omnipotent nature. It also involves the revelation of his ability and humanity. For example, we may picture Christ as a Good Shepherd, even a wise Rabbi, but would we take him with us into the boardroom or classroom? Would we take him with us to our family reunion? Can we picture him teaching a course on physics or psychology? In other words, is he relevant and our ultimate authority for everyday life?

Dallas Willard identifies this as a significant problem for discipleship:

What lies at the heart of the astonishing disregard of Jesus found in the moment-to-moment existence of multitudes of professing Christians, is a simple lack of respect for him. He is not seriously taken to be a person of great ability. But how, then, can we admire him? And what can devotion or worship mean if simple respect is not included in it? (The Great Omission p 19).

Not only must we respect Christ, but we must recognize his respect for us. Do we believe God sees us as worms or wonderful, vile or valuable, sinners or saints? The Psalmist reflects on the correct opinion God has of the people he created when he wrote, "What is man that you are mindful of him, the son of man that you care for him? You made him a little lower than the heavenly beings and crowned him with glory and honor" (Psalms 8:4-5)!

Part of our challenge in knowing Christ is to understand and embrace what God says is true about everyone who is part of his family of grace. John proclaims, "How great is the love the Father has lavished on us, that we should be called children of God" (1 John 3:1-2)! Like wow! Likewise, Paul reminds us frequently in his writings that we are beloved saints in the eyes of God. But do we share God's opinion?

Consistent dialogue

No friendship develops without a mutual, consistent conversation revealing what is on each person's mind and heart. Shut down dialogue, and you close down the relationship (as most married people know too well). Without consistent and mutual conversation with Christ, we may have good theology but a shallow relationship.

We usually understand that prayer and Scripture reading form this dialogue. He speaks to us through his Word, and we talk to him in prayer. The challenge is to develop this dialogue on a consistent and personal level. We must beware of treating Christ as only a "911" God we call on when we are in trouble and treating the Bible as a Chilton's Auto Manual, useful only when life breaks down.

Shared experiences

Friendships are developed one experience at a time because being together, sharing adventures, joys, heartaches, and sometimes just the daily routine builds a relationship. Shared experiences create a history of trust that can transcend time, as evidenced by membership in fraternities, sororities, military units, and sports teams. As we invite Christ into our daily narrative (both the pleasant and the challenging events), we strengthen the bridge of trust. This shared experience creates an awareness of his presence and is part of our abiding in him.

Brother Lawrence, in his book, *Practicing the Presence of God*, gives a helpful example of someone who included prayer and meditation into the everyday activities of his life. As a Carmelite friar living in a French monastery in the 17th century, Brother Lawrence used peeling potatoes' day-to-day work as an occasion for prayer and meditation on the Word. He believed every task was an opportunity to build his friendship with Christ.

Mutual transparency

Christ does not promise to share his heart with just casual observers. At the end of three and a half years of shared experiences, Jesus told his disciples:

I no longer call you servants...I have called you friends, for everything that I learned from my Father I have made known to you (John 15:15).

A study of how Jesus trained the twelve apostles reveals that Christ gradually revealed his heart as the disciples became closer to him. His first invitation to those early disciples was a casual invitation to, "Come and see." Over time and continued exposure, Christ gradually revealed his heart culminating in the Garden of Gethsemane, where they were given an in-depth and intimate look into the heart and passion of the Savior.

Conversely, we must also share our inner lives with Christ. David is the premier example in the Old Testament of a man after God's heart. In the Psalms he is brutally honest about how he felt and what he was thinking along with his faith in God's goodness.

Knowing Christ on the resurrection side of the cross is a fantastic privilege. The initiative and the means are a gift from him, but he waits for us to act, to open the door, and invite him into a relationship of knowing him, not just knowing facts about him.

For Reflection

1. Which of the four elements above need development in your relationship with Christ?

2. Is there a practical next step that comes to mind?

31

What's on the White Board?

The Lord GOD has given Me the tongue of disciples,
That I may know how to sustain the weary one with a word.
He awakens Me morning by morning,
He awakens My ear to listen as a disciple (Isa. 50:4).

A timeout is a critical tool for winning ball games. In basketball each team is allowed a limited amount. A coach calls a timeout for a variety of reasons:

- Thwart the momentum of the opposing team
- Refocus the players
- Set up a particular offense or defense
- Give the players a rest
- Overcome the crowd noise to send in instructions

Regardless of why, when a coach calls a timeout, the players huddle around him with their undivided attention. No one is on their cell phone, visiting with the cheerleaders, or talking with their friends. A coach has 60 seconds to get his ideas across. Coaches often explain their plan visually on a small whiteboard so players can see and not just hear the plan.

Jesus modeled and taught how to live in a relationship with the Father. The Gospels tell us that Jesus frequently responded to the Father's "timeout." One timeout Jesus took happened during a very successful healing "crusade" in Galilee. After a busy day with people, he slipped away to spend time with his Father. When he returned the next morning, he called a new play. Surprisingly, the new plan abandoned a thriving ministry in favor of moving on to other towns. The disciples were thinking, "If it ain't broke, don't fix it," but Jesus had gotten a new play on the whiteboard (Mark 1:32-39).

I consider my daily appointment with God (AWG) to be like a coach's timeout. It is a few minutes each day when I give my Coach my undivided attention. I have found that the first thing in the morning before there is too much crowd noise is the best time for me to hear his voice and understand what he is writing on the whiteboard.

I discover his "plays" when I allow Christ to speak his Word into my life consistently. Some days I feel like I'm playing offense while other days, I am on the defense. But each day I need his play.

My AWG is not a time for training or long explanations but a time for words of encouragement and clarity. There are times when I need to practice and train. The AWG is not a time for comprehensive Bible study; that's a different discipline. But each day I need a new word from my Coach.

A simple plan to see what's on the whiteboard could look like this:

- **Refocus**

Honestly admit the current state of your heart and mind. "This morning I'm so pumped I feel like I could climb Mt. Everest!" or "Right now my anxiety indicator is off the charts. I am redlining, and I don't know why – or maybe I do but don't want to admit it."

Next, refocus by reviewing some of the portraits of Christ that hang in the gallery of your mind. Finish the statement, "Lord, today I acknowledge that you are my _____" (Shepherd, Friend, Shelter, Healer, etc.)

- **Read**

As you go through a book of the Bible, read a short paragraph, several verses, or maybe a chapter, but keep it short. Read it over several times until a word or phrase stands out. Write it down in a journal, word for word from the text. In this part you are answering the question, "What does it say?"

- **Reflect**

Think about the meaning of what you just read, especially the words you just wrote down. Asking questions such as what, why, how, and when can help in this process. And most importantly, ask, "How is this relevant to my life?"

- **Record**

Write down your main reflection thoughts in a journal, keeping a log of what you hear God saying. Your journal is your whiteboard. Journaling clarifies and focuses your mind as you ask the Lord, "What is the one idea that you want me to reflect on today? What's the play of the day?"

- **Respond**

Pray back what you hear the Spirit saying to your heart. Prayer makes it a dialogue. Take what you have heard from God and pray that for others. Pray the "play" into reality.

You will need to initially give your AWG structure if it is to become a spiritual habit. Pick a time and place where you can be alone, undistracted, and consistent. Let your family know what you are doing so they can support your efforts.

You will probably need more than a 60-second timeout for a profitable AWG, but you don't need an hour. Start with 15 minutes until it becomes a pattern, then increase it as you have the opportunity. Initially, it may seem like you are performing a duty rather than personally meeting with the Lord. But once you master the mechanics, your focus will become more on your relationship with Christ rather than filling in an outline. At that point your AWG/timeout will change from a duty to delight.

As you develop your ear to hear from God, you will find it easier to share your whiteboard experiences with others as well. Sharing is different than preaching. Preaching uses the pronouns: you, they, them. Sharing uses personal pronouns: I, me, mine. By sharing what you are hearing from God, you may encourage others to take their timeout.

For Reflection

1. What is the next step for you to become consistent in a daily AWG?

2. What obstacles will you face? How will you overcome them?

Resources
for your spiritual journey

HighQuest Discipleship Series
(Men and Women)

The HighQuest series is a discipleship equipping platform and pathway that integrates personal reflection on Scripture with a small group experience.

This series is designed to equip men and women to walk with God for a lifetime by developing the personal spiritual practices that are foundational to living a Christ-centered life.

Biblical discipleship is not a course or a destination; it is a direction, a lifelong pursuit of Christ. HighQuest is built around the three major pursuits (tracks) of a disciple:

     I. Knowing Christ Deeply
     II. Reflecting Christ Authentically
     III. Sharing Christ Intentionally

These pursuits represent our vertical relationship with God, our inward, transformational relationship, and our outward relationship with others.

HighQuest is not a typical Bible study with questions to answer. It is a guided self-discovery approach that teaches men and women to feed themselves on Scripture. The primary spiritual practice that is foundational to each High-Quest unit is the daily appointment with God. Through this habit, a person learns how to hear God speak through his Word, reflect on what he hears, and apply it to his life.

(Available at www.highquest.info or www.highquest.biz)

Beginning the Walk
Ron and Mary Bennett

Following Jesus? Start Here.

Following Jesus isn't always clear cut. Fortunately, many people have walked the path ahead of us, and we can learn a lot from them.

Learn what you'll need from some of Jesus' earliest followers in this 18-lesson Bible study. Paul, John, and others will make sure you're ready for the journey. Beginning the Walk provides you the essentials you'll need along the way, including your identity in Christ, faith, the Word, prayer, community, grace, and the Holy Spirit's guidance.

There's no need to feel lost. Find the resources you need and stay focused on Christ -- every step of the way.

(Published by NavPress/Tyndale)

The Adventure of Disciplemaking
Ron Bennett and John Purvis

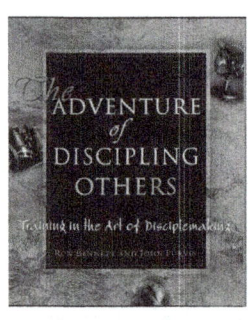

Jesus believed in the power of one. From the woman dawdling by the well to the tax collector dangling from a tree, Jesus called out and mentored the individual. He turned the beleaguered into the beautiful, the meager into the mighty, by pointing them to God and spotlighting their potential.

He knew one person could stir up the world and make a spiritual difference. Just like Jesus you can pour faith into believers, helping them grow spiritually and fulfill their unique niche in God's kingdom. With The Adventure of Discipling Others, anyone can mentor and love the process. Reading this book you'll cultivate a passion and develop the skill for life-to-life discipling and discover the amazing impact one life can have on another.

(Published by NavPress/Tyndale)

Intentional Disciplemaking
Ron Bennett

Cultivating a community of mature believers is essential to church growth. But how do you go about it? Offering a biblical, step-by-step strategy, Intentional Disciplemaking helps you develop solid followers of Christ. Learn to create a climate geared toward disciplemaking, reevaluate your outreach ministry, overcome barriers to faith, minister beyond your means, and more.

This book lays out what a biblical disciple of Christ looks like and how the church can create an environment geared toward making disciples and helping its people grow in spiritual maturity. Disciples don't just happen. They're developed through intentional planning and the efforts of a community of believers, one life at a time.

Intentional Disciplemaking gives the principles behind developing a disciple making community.

(Published by NavPress/Tyndale)

Blog
(www.rbennett.net)

I am writing this blog not as a theologian (although it will of necessity touch on theology) but as a practitioner. My passion is to understand and apply truth to life, especially as it relates to our calling to be and make disciples. It is a passion that has grown over years of living this incredible journey of faith and sharing that journey with others. This biblical, organic, and authentic journey of faith, while it may not be the average, should be the "normal" Christian life.

My intent is to take a fresh look at some old ideas, reexamining and reframing what we may be taking for granted, challenging some of the cultural baggage that has distort our view. I want to do this through the lens of "discipleship", specifically clarifying and applying its meaning and relevance in today's culture.

My invitation to you is to join me on this journey not as critics but as pioneers who are discovering the spiritual landscape of biblical discipleship.

Fire Resistant Parenting
Building Strong Homes in Today's Cultural Wildfires
Mary Bennett

Our families are in danger of wildfires that destroy not our physical houses but our spiritual lives and the lives of our loved ones. Surrounded by a culture that is suffering from a drought of truth and biblical values, our spiritual homes are being threatened. We need spiritually fire resistant homes that can stand against this cultural drought and protect the hearts and minds of our children.

The purpose of this Bible study is to discover Gods design for wise parenting and the process for intentionally creating an environment that will both promote that design and provide protection from the current fires in our culture.

In this study you will explore:

1. The biblical "blueprint" for the family with application for both parents and their children.

2. Some of the current cultural wildfires in order to gain the discernment needed to resist them. We cannot afford to be naïve. The awareness of the dangers along with the wisdom found in God's Word, are prerequisites for building a fire resistant home.

3. The critical materials and the process necessary for building a strong, fire resistant home. The objective truth of God's Word must be the basis for our faith and the faith of our children. In this study the metaphor of constructing a physically fire resistant house provides insight into that process.

The challenge for us as parents, grandparents, and educators (teachers within and without the church) is to equip the next generation with biblical truth that leads to lifelong, personal convictions. Only then will our children be able to stand against the cultural wildfires of today and tomorrow.

(Available on Amazon.com)

For additional copies of

Rethinking Discipleship
The Quest

can be ordered on Amazon.com

Coming next Year

Rethinking Discipleship
The Design

Made in the USA
Monee, IL
13 January 2021

57492363R00085